more than 100
SALADS
&
Salad Dressings

by Dr. Duane Lund

more than 100 SALADS & Salad Dressings

© **Copyright 2015**

By Lund S and R Publications, Staples, Minnesota 56479

First printing May 2015

Printed USA, etc.

ISBN-13: 978-0-9909370-0-5
ISBN-10: 0-9909370-0-3

Table of Contents

CHAPTER 1
Salads

CHAPTER 2
Salad Dressings

Salads

Boursin Steak Salad

Contributed by Lindsey Friesz

6 oz. sirloin steak
Mixed greens
Boursin cheese
Toasted pecans
Balsamic vinaigrette

Grill steak and let rest. Top greens with pecans. Place sliced steak on top of greens, then top with Boursin. Serve with balsamic vinaigrette.

Summer Berry Poppyseed Salad

Romaine
Strawberries
Blueberries
Candied pecans
Blue cheese crumbles
(For a delicious meal, serve with chicken)

Fill each plate with a mixture of Romaine and spinach. Top appropriately with remaining toppings.

Grilled Chicken Salad

½ t steak seasoning
½ t lemon-pepper seasoning
¼ t seasoned salt
½ lb. boneless skinless chicken breast*
2½ cups torn mixed salad greens
1 medium tomato, cut into thin wedges
¼ cup shredded carrot
¼ cup shredded cheddar cheese
⅓ cup chow mein noodles
¼ cup fat-free dressing of your choice
Cut into ½ inch strips

Mix the seasonings; rub over chicken. Grill on an indoor grill coated with nonstick cooking spray for 3-4 minutes or until juices run clear. In two bowls, arrange the greens, tomato, carrot, cheese and noodles. Top with chicken and dressing.

Serves two

Spinach Toss

¼ cup seasoned rice vinegar
⅛ cup vegetable oil
1 clove chopped garlic
1 package sliced mushrooms
1 cup sliced tomatoes
Blue cheese crumbles

In a large salad bowl, mix vinegar, garlic, salt and pepper. Add mushrooms and let sit for at least ½ hour right before serving. Add remaining ingredients and toss.

Honey-Zucchini Potato Salad

Small green pepper (chopped fine)
3 garlic cloves, chopped fine
2 T honey
2 T mustard
2 T mayonnaise
3 T olive oil
2 pounds zucchini halved length-wise
½ pound potatoes, quartered
2 hard-boiled eggs, peeled and chopped
½ cup sweet pickles

Whisk together pepper, honey, garlic, mustard, mayonnaise, and oil. Season with salt and pepper. Save half for dressing. Brush the pieces of zucchini with remaining jalapeño mixture.

Grill on an oiled rack of a covered grill 7 minutes, turning once. Meanwhile, cook potatoes in salted water 10 minutes or until tender; drain. Coarsely chop zucchini and combine with other ingredients. Season with salt and pepper, top with parsley.

Corn & Cantaloupe Chopped Salad

2 cups fresh corn kernels
½ cantaloupe, small cubes (2 cups)
½ red pepper
½ cup diced red onion
2 T fresh dill
2 T olive oil
1 T dry mustard
1 cup spring greens (mixed)

Cook corn in salted water (boiling) for 2 minutes. Drain and rinse until cool. In a bowl, place cantaloupe, red pepper, onion and dill.

Toss to combine.

Combine lemon juice, olive oil and mustard in a bowl. Pour over corn mixture.
Stir. Season with salt (to taste). Add greens and toss. Let stand 5 minutes before serving.

Steak & Noodle Salad

4 oz. noodles
2 T vinegar
2 T olive oil (divided)
½ pound steak of your choosing
Salt and pepper
4 oz. mushroom caps (no stems)

4 oz. peas
2 garlic cloves, thinly sliced
1 red chili (sliced thin)
2 t fresh ginger, finely chopped
½ cup fresh cilantro

Cook the noodles according to directions on package. Drain and rinse under cold water. Place in a bowl and toss with vinegar.

Heat 1 T oil in a skillet medium-high heat. Season steak with salt and pepper

Cook on each side to desired doneness (about 4 minutes). Transfer to a cool surface and let rest 5 minutes, then slice.

Wipe out skillet and heat remaining 1 T of oil over medium heat. Add mushrooms and cook, tossing occasionally for 3 minutes. Add peas, garlic, chili, ginger and a dash of salt and pepper. Toss until peas are tender. (About 3 minutes)

Toss the noodles with the above.

Blt - Stuffed Tomatoes

4 large tomatoes
1¾ cups cooked wild rice
4 oz. bacon, diced
⅓ cup walnuts, chopped fine
3 T mayonnaise
3 T yogurt (nonfat)
½ cup parsley (fresh)
2 dashes pepper (black)
Dash of salt
8 cups chopped romaine
1 T olive oil (virgin)
1 T vinegar
Bread or toast of your choosing

Cut the top 1/5 off each tomato and scoop out the flesh.

Heat wild rice for 3 minutes in a micro-safe bowl. Stir in the bacon and heat 2 more minutes.

Stir in walnuts, mayonnaise, yogurt, parsley, pepper and a dash of salt. Scoop rice mixture into tomatoes; replace tops.

Toss romaine with oil, vinegar and a pinch of salt. Serve with bread or toast.

Minted Cucumber & Tomato Salad

4 T vinegar
4 T sugar
Dash of salt
Dash of pepper
1 large cucumber (peeled, seeded, ½ inch thick)
4 tomatoes, chopped (¾ inch pieces)
2 T diced onion (red)
2 T chopped fresh mint

Combine vinegar, sugar, salt and pepper.
Combine remaining ingredients, (in a separate bowl)

Add dressing to cucumber and tomatoes (stir well).

Refrigerate at least 30 minutes before serving.

Serves four

Summer Corn Salad

6 large ears of corn, husked and cleaned
1 large onion, chopped fine
¼ cup fresh basil, chopped fine
1 tomato (large, chopped)
¼ cup olive oil
3 T vinegar (white)
Dash of salt
Dash of pepper

Cut the kernels off of the cobs; use a sharp knife.

In a large enough bowl, toss together all ingredients. Refrigerate. Serve cold.

Serves six

Bulgur, Vegetable & Watercress Salad

1 cup coarse bulgur*
1 cup water or vegetable broth (no salt)
3 cups chickpeas, drained and rinsed
   (no salt)
1 medium cucumber, peeled and cut
   (dice-size)
½ pint cherry size tomatoes cut in half
1 green onion, peeled and cut thin

1 T white miso paste
1 T toasted sesame oil
¼ cup rice vinegar
3 T vegetable oil
2 T honey
2 cups fresh watercress leaves
Flesh of one avocado, cut into cubes
*May substitute whole wheat couscous

Combine the bulgur and broth or water in a medium bowl and let sit for at least 90 minutes at room temperature, or refrigerate overnight. (If using whole wheat couscous, it will be ready in about 45 minutes or refrigerate overnight.) When ready to serve, fluff the bulgur with a fork. Add the chickpeas, cucumber, tomatoes and scallion and toss.

Divide the watercress leaves among salad plates. Drizzle with the remaining dressing. Mound some of the bulgur mixture on top of each portion.

Add the avocado and serve.

Sweet Bell Pepper & Onion Salad

1½ pounds orange or yellow bell peppers
1 small red onion, thinly sliced into rings
2 T sherry or red wine vinegar
Dash each of salt and pepper
¼ cup coarsely chopped fresh basil
¼ cup chopped fresh chives
¼ cup coarsely chopped flat leaf parsley
¼ cup freshly chopped fresh mint
2 T olive oil

Toss bell peppers, onion and vinegar in a large bowl; season with a dash each of salt and pepper. Let sit until bell peppers are slightly softened (10 to 20 minutes).

Just before serving, toss herbs and oil with bell pepper mixture.

Corn & Zucchini Salad with Feta

5 ears of corn, husked
Dash of salt (preferably kosher)
4 small zucchini (about 1½ pounds total)
A dozen zucchini blossoms (torn into large pieces)
¼ cup fresh basil (coarsely chopped)
¼ cup fresh flat leaf parsley, coarsely chopped
½ cup olive oil
¼ cup vinegar (wine)
½ T pepper (freshly ground)
1 cup feta, crumbled

Cook corn in a pot of boiling, salted water until bright yellow and tender; about 3 minutes. Transfer to a plate and let cool.

Cut kernels from the cobs and place in a bowl. Add zucchini, zucchini blossoms, basil, oil, parsley, vinegar, and red pepper flakes; toss. Serve topped with feta.

Tomato, Onion & Roasted Lemon Salad

1 lemon, sliced lengthwise, thinly sliced, seeds removed
1 T thinly sliced fresh sage leaves
1 T sugar
2 T olive oil (divided)
1 T pomegranate molasses
½ T ground allspice and 1 dash each of salt and pepper
1½ pounds of small tomatoes
½ small red onion, sliced thin
½ cup fresh flat-leaf parsley leaves
¼ cup fresh mint leaves (torn if large)
¼ cup purple sprouts or small greens

Preheat oven to 325 degrees.

Cook lemon slices in a pan of hot water (boiling) for 2 minutes. Drain and pat dry.
In a bowl, toss lemon slices with sage, sugar, and 1 T oil. Spread out on a parchment-lined baking sheet and bake until lemons are no longer wet (only slightly colored about 15 minutes) and let cool.

Whisk pomegranate molasses, allspice and 1 T of oil in a bowl. Add dash each of salt and pepper. Add onions, tomatoes, onion, parsley, mint and sprouts. Toss with a dash each of salt and pepper.

Taco Pasta Salad

1 pound lean ground beef (hamburger)
1 pkg. (1¼ oz. taco seasoning)
½ cup kernels from an ear of corn
½ cup chopped zucchini
1 cup Mexican blend cheese
2 cups rigatoni pasta (follow pkg. directions)

Brown the hamburger in a skillet over medium-high heat until no longer pink
(8 to 10 minutes).

Drain and stir in taco seasoning, corn, zucchini, salsa and Mexican cheese.
Serve over pasta and garnish as you please.

Serves six

Six Jars of Layered Salad

6 pint-size glass jars
½ chopped onion
1 can (15 oz.) black beans, rinsed & drained
1 cup chicken broth (low sodium)
1 T salt (divided)
1 garlic clove, minced
¾ cup Greek yogurt
2 T olive oil (extra virgin) divided

8 oz cheddar cheese (shredded)
½ cup mayonnaise
1 jar pimientos, drained (4 oz.)
Pepper (freshly ground)
½ cucumber, chopped
½ T lemon juice
1 pint small tomatoes, halved
Bagel chips for serving (optional)

In a sauce pan, combine onion, beans, broth, and ½ t salt. Bring to a boil, then lower to a simmer and cook, stirring occasionally until thickened (about 15 minutes) Remove from heat.

Smear together garlic and ½ t salt. (To form a paste) Whisk into yogurt with 1 T olive oil.

Combine cheese, mayonnaise and pimientos in a food processor. Season with pepper. Toss cucumber in a bowl with remaining 1 T of oil, lemon juice, salt and pepper to taste.

Spoon ½ cup of bean mixture into each of 6 jars. Layer each with 2½ T pimento cheese, ⅓ cup cucumbers, and 2 T garlic yogurt. Top with tomatoes, divided between jars. Close jars and serve with a fork (and bagel chips – if desired).

Watermelon & Grilled Cheese Salad

6 oz. halloumi or mozzarella cheese (drained)
3 cups arugula
¼ watermelon (seedless) in small wedges
3 T extra virgin olive oil
Aged balsamic vinegar
1 bunch fresh mint, chopped
¼ cup pistachios, chopped (roughly)

Slice cheese into 1/3 inch slices. Heat a grill or grill pan to medium-high; brush grate with olive oil. Grill cheese about 2 minutes on each side until grill marks show.

Place arugula on a platter; top with watermelon and cheese. Drizzle with olive oil and vinegar. Scatter mint and pistachios on top.

Squash & Farro Salad

1½ pounds diced butternut squash (¼-¾ inch)
4 T olive oil
1 T salt
½ T black pepper
1 small rotisserie chicken
1½ cups Nature's Earthly Choice parboiled farro
½ cup sweetened, dried cranberries

½ t ground cumin
½ t ground ginger
½ t ground cinnamon
¼ cup cider vinegar
2 t Dijon mustard
1 t honey
2 cups baby kale,, shredded
½ cup crumbled goat cheese
⅓ cup toasted walnuts, chopped

Heat oven to 450 degrees. Toss diced squash with 2 T of the oil and 1 dash each of salt and pepper and spread onto a large rimmed baking sheet. Roast at 450 degrees for 20 minutes, stirring halfway through. Cool to room temp. Meanwhile, remove and discard skin from chicken. Shred meat into pieces (about 3 cups). Refrigerate overnight.

The next evening, combine farro, a dash of salt and 4½ cups of water. Boil in a large pot for 20 minutes. Stir in cranberries; boil 5 more minutes. In a skillet, combine cumin ginger, cinnamon and a dash each of salt and pepper. Toast 1 minute.

Whisk together vinegar, mustard, honey and 2 t oil. Whisk into skillet with seasonings. Reheat squash and chicken in microwave (2 minutes)

Combine ingredients in a serving bowl. Drizzle with dressing, toss and sprinkle with goat cheese and walnuts. Serve at room temp.

Pork Tenderloin Salad

24 oz. baby red potatoes
2 T olive oil
½ T salt
½ T pepper
1 canned chipotle in adobo, chopped *
1 T mayonnaise
2½ t Dijon mustard

2 t oregano, chopped
1¼ pounds pork tenderloin
3 T red wine vinegar
1 T honey
1 pkg. salad greens (5 oz.)
1 pear, cored and diced
Plus 2 T adobo

Heat the oven to 425 degrees the night before. Toss the potatoes with 1 T of the oil, and a dash each of salt and pepper. Spread onto a rimmed sheet. Blend together chipotle, 1 t adobo, the 2 t mustard, 1 t oregano, and 1 dash each salt and pepper. Brush onto pork tenderloin on a rimmed baking sheet.

Roast and stir potatoes at 425 degrees for 35 minutes. Remove from oven and cover pork with a foil. Cool pork and potatoes and refrigerate overnight.

Meanwhile, whisk together vinegar, 1 t remaining oil, dash of salt, 1 t adobo, 1 t oregano and honey. Wrap and store overnight.

At dinnertime, toss together roasted potatoes, salad greens, diced pear and dressing. Divide among 4 bowls and fan thin slices of pork on top.

Chicken & Napa Cabbage Salad

2 T fresh lime juice
2 T sesame oil (Asian)
½ t salt
½ t pepper
5 cups Napa cabbage, sliced thin
2 cups cooked, skinless chicken breast (shredded)
1 cup carrots (cut match-stick size)
1 green bell pepper, sliced thin
2 scallions, thinly sliced (diagonally)

Whisk together lime juice, sesame oil, and one dash each salt and pepper in a large serving bowl.

Add cabbage, chicken, carrots, bell pepper

And scallions and toss to coat.

Serves four

Rice Salad with Fava Beans & Pistachios

½ cup wild rice
Dash kosher salt
1 cup basmati rice
1 dried lime
1 cup fresh shelled fava beans
½ cup chopped fresh dill

½ cup fresh flat-leaf parsley (chopped)
½ cup unsalted, raw pistachios
¼ cup olive oil
2 t finely grated lemon zest
¼ cup lemon juice
½ t grated lime zest

Cook wild rice in a medium pot of boiling water until tender and grains start to split. (35 to 40 minutes.) Drain and let cool.

Meanwhile, combine basmati rice, lime, and 1½ cups of water in a medium saucepan, season with salt and bring to a boil. Reduce heat, cover and simmer 10 minutes. Remove from heat and fluff with a fork. Cover, let sit until water is absorbed (about 5 minutes) Let cool; discard lime.

If using fresh fava beans, cook in a saucepan of boiling salted water about 4 minutes. Drain; transfer to a bowl of ice water; drain and peel.

Toss wild rice, basmati rice, parsley, pistachios, oil, lemon juice and zest, lime powder, and fava beans in a bowl, season with salt.

Parsley, Red Onion & Pomegranate Salad

1 large red onion, thinly sliced
2 T sugar
1 T ground sumac
Salt (preferably kosher)
3 T olive oil
1 T red wine vinegar
1 T honey
4 cups lightly packed fresh flat-leaf Parsley leaves with tender stems
¼ cup pomegranate seeds

Toss onion, sugar and sumac in a medium bowl; season with salt and let sit 30 minutes. Add oil, vinegar, and pomegranate molasses and toss to combine. Let sit 5 minutes.

Just before serving, toss in parsley and pomegranate seeds. Season with salt.

Shaved Honeydew, Fennel & Olive Salad

1 T orange zest, finely grated
1 T fresh orange juice
2 T fresh lemon juice
2 T olive oil (plus more for drizzling)
1½ pounds honeydew melon*
½ fennel bulb, shaved
2 T coarsely chopped fennel fronds
¼ cup brined green olives, pitted & coarsely chopped
rinds and seeds removed; shaved on a mandolin

Whisk orange juice, lemon juice, and season with 1 dash each of salt and pepper.

Add melon, shaved fennel and olives to vinaigrette and toss to coat. Top salad with orange zest and fennel fronds. Drizzle with more oil and season with salt and pepper.

Prosciutto & Arugula Salad

1 pound Italian bow-tie pasta
¼ pound unsalted butter (room temp.)
1½ cups loosely packed baby arugula
1½ cups cooked peas
4 oz. prosciutto, torn into bite-size pieces
3 cups Parmigiano cheese *
4 ripe small tomatoes, seeded and diced
3 T chives, finely chopped
3 t basil leaves, chopped fine
salt and pepper to taste
plus additional for serving

Cook pasta in a large pot of boiling salted water for eight minutes. Drain the pasta, reserving a cup of pasta water.

Transfer pasta into a warmed serving bowl. Immediately add the butter, peas, arugula, prosciutto, cheese and tomatoes. Gradually add 3 t of the reserved pasta water. Continue to add water until the sauce turns creamy.

Add the chives and basil, and toss again. Season with salt and pepper to taste.

Refrigerate before serving.

Tomato, Pickled Melon & Burrata Salad

2 t white wine vinegar
Dash of kosher salt
¼ t pepper (set aside more)
1 pound watermelon, rind removed (sliced and aligned into thin rounds)
12 oz. fresh burrata or mozzarella, torn
Olive oil (for drizzling)
Fresh basil leaves for serving
Flaky sea salt, such as Maldon

Combine vinegar, kosher salt, dash of pepper, and 2 T of water in a large bowl; add melon and toss to coat. Let stand at room temperature at least 30 minutes.

Remove melon from pickling liquid and arrange on a platter with tomato and burrata. Drizzle with oil and some pickling liquid, top with basil, and season with sea salt and pepper.

Do ahead: Melon can be pickled 2 hours ahead. Cover and chill.

Organic Baby Lettuces & Quinoa Salad

3 T extra virgin olive oil
1 T balsamic vinegar
1 T Dijon mustard
Dash of salt
Dash of pepper
6 cups baby organic lettuce
1 cup cooked quinoa, cooled
2 cups corn kernels (about 2 ears)
1 cup blanched snow peas
2 cups small tomatoes, halved
1 avocado, diced
1 small red onion, thinly sliced
½ cup shaved parmesan

Place oil, vinegar, 1 T water, mustard, salt and pepper in a small lidded jar. Shake until combined.

In a large salad bowl, combine lettuce, quinoa, corn, snow peas, tomatoes, avocado and onion. Toss with dressing and top with parmesan. Serve immediately.

Greens & Grain Salad

1 6 oz. container plain, fat-free yogurt
2 T white wine vinegar
1 cup fresh dill, chopped
1 T sugar
Dash or two of salt
Dash or two of pepper
1 cup frozen fully cooked wheat berries
1 cup cooked lentils
1 pkg. cooked beets (8.8 oz.) diced
8 cups chopped butter lettuce
8 cups baby spinach
½ cup pistachios (unsalted)
1 6 oz. can salmon

Stir together yogurt, vinegar, dill, sugar, salt, and pepper. Set aside.

Heat berries in a micro-safe bowl for 2 minutes, stir and heat 1 more minute (until thawed).

Toss wheat berries, lentils, beets, lettuce, spinach, and pistachios in a bowl with dressing. If desired, gently fold in salmon.

Wax Bean & Radish Salad with Parsley Dressing

¼ cup low-fat buttermilk
¼ cup reduced fat yogurt
2 T fresh flat-leaf parsley, chopped fine
1½ T fresh lemon juice
1 T shallots chopped fine
1½ T Dijon mustard
Dash of kosher salt
8 cups of water

1 pound yellow wax beans (fresh)
1 cup radishes, thinly sliced
1 T olive oil (extra virgin)
¼ cup crumbled blue cheese
¼ t black pepper
3 center cut bacon slices, cooked, drained and crumbled

Combine first 7 ingredients in a small bowl.

Bring 8 cups of water to a boil in a large saucepan; add wax beans; cook 5 minutes or until crisp-tender. Drain and plunge into ice water – drain. Combine beans, radishes, and oil in a large bowl; toss to coat. Place bean mixture on a serving platter; drizzle with buttermilk dressing. Top with cheese, pepper and bacon.

Kale & Beet Salad

1 cup torn mint leaves
⅓ cup red onion, sliced vertically
1 pkg. baby kale (6 oz.)
¼ cup Greek yogurt, 2% reduced fat, plain
2 T buttermilk, fat free
2 T white wine vinegar
1½ T olive oil (extra virgin)
¼ T kosher salt
¼ T black pepper
4 hard-cooked eggs (large) quartered lengthwise
1 8 oz. pkg. baby beets, quartered, peeled and steamed
½ cup walnuts, coarsely chopped
½ cup blue cheese, crumbled

Combine mint, onion and kale in a large bowl. Combine yogurt, buttermilk, vinegar, oil, salt and pepper in a bowl, stirring with a whisk. Drizzle yogurt mixture over kale mixture; toss gently to coat.

Arrange eggs and beets over salad; sprinkle with nuts and cheese.

Thai - Style Pork Salad

1 cup unsweetened coconut milk
1 cup snipped fresh cilantro
⅓ cup soy sauce, reduced sodium
¼ cup lime juice
1 T fresh ginger, grated
1 pound boneless pork loin in bite-size pieces
1 T olive oil
1 cup fresh, green beans, sliced on the bias
1 cup shredded carrots
12 Napa cabbage leaves, cilantro leaves, lime wedges

Combine coconut milk, cilantro, soy sauce, lime juice, and ginger in a large bowl.
Add pork. Toss to coat.

In a large skillet, heat oil over medium high heat. Add meat mixture.

Cook 3 minutes. Add green beans.
Cook and stir 3 or 4 minutes until beans are crisp tender and pork is just slightly pink, stirring
occasionally. Add carrots just before serving.

Serves four

To serve, top cabbage leaves with pork mixture. Sprinkle with
additional cilantro and serve with lime wedges.

Green Bean & Tomato Salad with Buttermilk Dressing

½ cup buttermilk
2 T fresh lemon juice
½ T garlic powder
½ T onion powder
3 T olive oil, divided
Kosher salt
black pepper

1 pound of green or wax beans, trimmed
2 large leeks; white and green parts only*
1 pint small tomatoes, halved
1 large tomato, sliced
½ cup fresh mint leaves, sliced thin
¼ cup fresh chives, chopped
*halved and cut into 4 inch pieces

Whisk buttermilk, lemon juice, garlic powder, onion powder, and 1 T oil in a small bowl; season with salt and pepper.

Cook beans in a large pot of boiling salted water until just tender, about 3 minutes. Using a slotted spoon, transfer to a colander set in a bowl of ice water; drain. Place beans in a large bowl.

Return water in a pot to a boil and cook leeks until just tender (about 3 minutes); drain. Transfer a colander to ice water; drain and add to bowl with beans.

Add small tomatoes and remaining 2 T of oil and toss to combine; season with salt and pepper.

Serve salad over large tomato slices drizzled with buttermilk dressing and topped with mint and chives.

Peach Caprese Salad

3 large peaches, sliced
3 balls fresh mozzarella, sliced
10–12 fresh basil leaves, whole with stems removed
¼ cup extra virgin olive oil
1 T kosher salt
2 dashes of pepper

Slice the peaches and fresh mozzarella between ⅛ and ¼ inch thick, but not more than ¼ inch. On a plate or platter, begin layering with a slice of peach first, followed by a slice of mozzarella and then a basil leaf (the basil stands out better with a white background). Repeat this patter, until finished.

Once the layering is complete, sprinkle the salt and pepper evenly over the entire salad, then drizzle the olive oil back and forth over the layers. Lightly drizzle with balsamic reduction*— the flavor is intense and a little goes a long way. For added flavor, sprinkle toasted almond slices on top of the salad.

*balsamic reduction means 2 cups of balsamic vinegar.

Serves four to six

Layered Veggie Tortellini Salad

1 pkg. frozen cheese tortellini (16 oz.)
2 cups broccoli florets
2 cups cherry (small) tomatoes
2 celery ribs, chopped (fine)
1 can (2¼ oz.) black olives, sliced and drained
1 cup cheddar cheese, shredded
¾ cup mayonnaise
3 T grated Parmesan cheese
2 T lemon juice
2 T heavy whipping cream
1 T dried thyme

Cook tortellini according to package directions, drain and rinse in cold water.

In a 2½ quart glass bowl, layer the tortellini, tomatoes, celery, broccoli, olives and cheddar cheese.

To prepare dressing. Whisk together parmesan, mayo, lemon juice, cream and thyme. Spoon over salad. Cover and refrigerate until serving time.

Layered Tomato - Watermelon Salad

5 T extra-virgin olive oil
1½ T red wine vinegar
8 cups seedless watermelon diced into 1½ in. chunks
3 T assorted fresh herbs, chopped
1 T coarse kosher salt, divided (or to taste)
About 3 pounds large, red tomatoes, ½ in. chunks
5 oz. feta cheese, crumbled
1 cup sprouts, such as sunflower or alfalfa
5 cups arugula
½ cup sunflower seeds, toasted lightly

In a one-cup glass measure, whisk together oil and vinegar.

In a large bowl, toss the watermelon with half the oil-vinegar mixture, 1½ T assorted herbs and ¼ T salt.

In another bowl, toss the tomatoes with the remaining oil-vinegar mixture, 1½ T herbs and ¼ t salt.

In a clear glass bowl, layer watermelon, tomatoes, feta cheese, sprouts, arugula, and sunflower seeds.

Layered Spinach Salad

¾ pound of spinach
1 medium-size cucumber, sliced thin
½ cup radishes, sliced thin
¼ cup thinly sliced green onions
½ cup prepared ranch dressing
5 slices of crisp bacon, crumbled
½ cup peanuts

Remove and discard spinach stems. Rinse leaves well; drain and pat dry. Tear spinach into bite-size pieces and arrange evenly in a large bowl.

Evenly layer cucumber slices, radishes, and green onions. Spread dressing over top.

Cover and chill up to 24 hours. Just before serving, sprinkle with bacon and peanuts.

Individual Layered Salads with Orange Ginger Dressing

1 cup uncooked wheat berries, rinsed
Pinch of salt
1 cup uncooked quinoa, rinsed
1½ cups diced green bell pepper, divided
1½ cups diced red bell pepper, divided
1½ cups shredded carrots, divided
1 pkg. edamame, divided (12 oz.)

⅔ cup freshly squeezed orange juice
⅓ cup apple juice
1 T apple cider vinegar
1 T ginger (minced)
1 T lime juice
¼ T kosher salt

In a medium pot, combine rinsed berries, 3½ cups of water, and a pinch of salt. Bring to a rolling boil, reduce heat, cover and simmer about 1 hour.

In another medium pot, add quinoa and 2 cups of water. Bring to a boil reduce heat to low, cover and simmer until fluffy, about 20 minutes.

When the grains have cooked, add into each mason jar: ½ cup cooked wheat berries, ¼ cup green pepper, ¼ cup red pepper, ½ cup quinoa, ½ cup carrots, and ½ cup edamame. Push the ingredients down in the jar after adding the quinoa and edamame. Repeat with the remaining jars.

For the dressing, whisk together the orange juice, apple juice, vinegar, ginger, lime juice and salt. Spoon over salads.

Healthy Seven Layer Salad with Avocado Dressing

1 pkg. spring lettuce mix (10 oz.)
1 pkg. garbanzo beans, drained and rinsed (15 oz.)
2 medium red bell peppers, diced
1 cup halved small tomatoes (cherry size)
1 cup mozzarella cheese, shredded
6 slices of turkey bacon, cooked and crumbled
1 avocado
1 cup Greek yogurt (plain)
2 T lemon juice
½ T garlic, minced
Dash of salt
2 T honey

In a large glass bowl or trifle dish, layer lettuce, beans, peppers, and tomatoes.

Refrigerate several hours.

Before serving, add layers of cheese and bacon.

To make dressing, blend together avocado, yogurt, lemon juice, garlic, salt, and honey until smooth. Spoon over salad.

Inger's Seven Layer Fruit Salad

3 cups watermelon, diced
7 T sugar, divided
2 cups green grapes, halved
1½ cups cherries, pitted and halved
2 peaches, diced
2 cups blueberries
2 cups diced honeydew melon
2 cups diced strawberries

Place the watermelon on the bottom of a large clear bowl or trifle dish; sprinkle with 1 T sugar.

Layer grapes on top and sprinkle with 1 T sugar.

Repeat the process of sprinkling the sugar as you layer the cherries, peaches, blueberries, melon and strawberries.

Refrigerate several hours before serving.

Red Quinoa Salad with Black Beans & Avocado

1 cup red quinoa
2 cups water
2 T freshly squeezed lime juice
2 T light-tasting oil*
½ t of salt
½ T ground cumin

½ cup finely minced red onion
1½ cups cooked black beans, rinsed and drained
1 fresh avocado, coarsely chopped
¼ cup minced cilantro

such as sunflower, canola or soybean oil

Rinse quinoa well, then put it in a saucepan and bring to a boil. Reduce to a simmer, cook until all water is absorbed (about 15 minutes). The quinoa is done when the grain appears soft and the red becomes translucent. The germ ring will be visible along the outside edge of the grain.

Allow to cool to room temperature.
While quinoa is cooking, prepare dressing: Whisk together lime juice, oil, salt and cumin.
Toss cooked quinoa with onion, black beans, avocado and cilantro. Add dressing and toss until evenly distributed.
Serve at room temperature.

Rainbows & Butterflies Pasta Salad

8 oz. bow-tie pasta, preferably whole grain
3 T plus 1 t extra virgin olive oil, divided
1 cup corn kernels, thawed if frozen
1 cup shelled edamame, thawed if frozen
1 medium red bell pepper, diced
2 medium carrots, shredded, about ½ cup
⅓ cup grated parmesan cheese (about 1 oz.)
¼ t of salt or to taste

Cook the pasta as the label directs. Drain and toss with 1 t olive oil to prevent sticking; let cool.

In a large bowl, toss cooled pasta with the corn, edamame, bell pepper and carrots. Drizzle with the remaining 3 T of olive oil and toss to coat. Add the parmesan and salt; toss again and season to taste.

Chicken Salad Roll-ups

1 cup chopped, cooked chicken
1 celery ribs, diced
1 T mayonnaise
1 t Dijon mustard
2 t lemon juice
Dash of salt
4 slices whole-wheat sandwich bread

In a bowl, combine chicken, celery, mayonnaise, Dijon, lemon juice, and salt and toss to mix well.

Using a rolling pin, roll the bread to ¼ inch thick.

Spread ¼ cup of the chicken salad mixture on each slice of bread and roll it up.
(It may be secured with a rubber band.)

Mexican Seven-Layer Salad

4 cups chopped lettuce
1 cup chopped tomato (large)
½ cup chopped green onion
1 (15½ oz) black beans, rinsed and drained
1 cup cheddar cheese, shredded
1 cup salsa
1 cup tortilla chips (crushed)

Layer lettuce, tomato, green onion, beans, cheese, and salsa in a large bowl or trifle dish.
Refrigerate until ready to serve. Before serving, top with crushed tortilla chips.

Serves eight

Blueberry, Beet & Basil Summer Salad

4 cups small yellow beets, halved (about 8)
1 lemon
1 cup blueberries, fresh
1 cup arugula
2 cups fresh basil leaves
1 medium fennel bulb, trimmed, cored and slice thin
1 medium red onion, sliced
1 6-oz. carton plain Greek yogurt
1 T honey
1 T chopped fresh flat-leaf Italian parsley
1 t crushed red pepper
1 T olive oil

Cook beets in lightly salted boiling water 15 minutes or until tender. Drain; cool. Remove skins from beets. Cut into wedges. Shred the peel of the lemon (finely). Juice the lemon; set aside.

In a large bowl, combine beets, blueberries, arugula, basil leaves, fennel, onion and reserved lemon juice. For dressing, in a small bowl, stir together yogurt, lemon peel, honey and crushed red pepper. Whisk in olive oil. Serve dressing with salad.

Serves six

Vegetable Rice Salad

1½ cups long grain white rice
1 red bell pepper, seeded and chopped
1 English cucumber, diced (medium size)
1 pint grape (small) tomatoes, halved
½ small red onion (diced)
½ cup walnuts – chopped
2 stalks celery, chopped
3 green onions, sliced

2 T chopped fresh basil
2 T chopped fresh parsley
⅓ cup canola oil
1 lime, zested and juiced
3 T rice wine vinegar
2 T light brown sugar
Kosher salt
Pepper, freshly ground

Cook rice according to directions on the package. Remove from heat, let stand 5 minutes and fluff with a fork.

Transfer rice to a large bowl. Add bell pepper and next 7 ingredients; toss well.

Whisk together oil and next 3 ingredients in a small bowl. Season to taste with salt and pepper. Drizzle dressing over rice mixture; toss well.

Quick Rice Salad

3 cups leftover rice
⅓ cup Italian dressing*
2 large tomatoes, chopped
1 cucumber, peeled, seeded and chopped
½ red onion, chopped
½ cup parsley, chopped

Combine all ingredients in a bowl. Toss well.

Serves six

Kale, Quinoa & Cherry Salad

3 t extra virgin olive oil
3 T cider vinegar
1 T honey
2 t Dijon mustard
¼ t black pepper
¼ t kosher salt
1½ 6 oz. pkgs. baby kale
1½ 8.5 oz. pkgs. precooked quinoa & brown rice blend
¾ cup fresh, sweet cherries, pitted and halved
⅔ cup fresh chopped flat-leaf parsley
⅓ cup shallots, sliced thin
1 (15 oz.) can unsalted chickpeas, rinsed and drained
2 oz. goat cheese, crumbled (about ½ cup)

Combine first 6 ingredients in a medium bowl. Combine 1½ T oil mixture and kale.

Place kale mixture on a platter. Stir quinoa blend, cherries, parsley, shallots, and chickpeas into remaining oil mixture. Top kale mixture with quinoa mixture and cheese.

Serves six

Crab & Heirloom Tomato Salad

⅓ cup fresh cilantro leaves
4 mini sweet bell peppers; thinly sliced diagonally
1 large shallot, thinly sliced
1 jalapeño pepper, thinly sliced diagonally
12 oz. jumbo lump crab meat, shell removed
2½ T canola mayonnaise
1 t grated lime rind
1 T fresh lime juice
2 pounds heirloom tomatoes, sliced
1½ T extra virgin olive oil
¼ t kosher salt
¼ t freshly ground black pepper
¼ cup small fresh basil leaves

Combine first 5 ingredients in a large bowl. Combine mayonnaise, rind and juice in a small bowl, stirring with a whisk. Add mayonnaise mixture to crab mixture. Toss gently to coat. Arrange tomatoes on a serving platter; drizzle with oil. Sprinkle tomatoes with salt and pepper. Mound crab mixture over tomatoes. Sprinkle with basil leaves.

Greek Shrimp Salad

SALSA:

2 ripe avocados, peeled, pitted and diced
1 tomato, steamed, seeded and finely diced
1 jalapeño pepper, stemmed, seeded
  and minced
1 cup finely chopped red onion
1 garlic clove, minced
2 T fresh lime juice
1 T finely chopped fresh cilantro
½ t ground cumin
½ t salt

NACHOS:

8 oz. tortilla chips
3 cups shredded Monterey Jack cheese
¾ pound medium shrimp, grilled or sautéed
2 green onions, white and green parts
  thinly sliced
½ cup cilantro leaves, loosely packed

To prepare salsa, place all ingredients in a medium bowl, stir to combine.

Preheat oven broiler. Spread tortilla chips in a 13 x 9 inch baking pan. Spread half the cheese over chips. Arrange shrimp over cheese and sprinkle remaining cheese over shrimp. Broil about 6 inches from heat source until the cheese is bubbly and melted, 3 to 5 minutes. Remove from oven and drop spoonsful of salsa over nachos. Sprinkle green onions and fresh cilantro all over. Serve immediately.

Serves eight

Fresh Broccoli Salad with Lemon

¼ cup cider vinegar
¼ cup lemon juice
½ cup reduced fat mayonnaise
¼ cup sugar
2 T prepared mustard
1 t garlic salt
⅛ t pepper
6 oz. cream cheese, softened
14 cups fresh small broccoli florets (about 2 ¼ pounds)
12 oz. fresh mushrooms, stems removed, chopped
16 bacon strips, cooked and crumbled
1 cup raisins
⅓ cup chopped red onion
Lemon wedges (optional)

Place cider, lemon juice, mayonnaise, sugar, prepared mustard, garlic salt, pepper, and cream cheese in a blender, cover and process until smooth.

In a large bowl, combine broccoli, mushrooms, bacon, raisins, and onion. Pour dressing over salad; toss to coat. Refrigerate until serving. Serve with lemon wedges if desired.

Chilled Shrimp Pasta Salad

3 cups small pasta shells (uncooked)
½ cup sour cream
½ cup mayonnaise
¼ cup horseradish sauce
2 T grated onion
1½ t seasoned salt
¾ t pepper
1 lb, peeled and deveined cooked small shrimp
1 large cucumber, seeded and chopped
3 celery ribs, thinly sliced
Red lettuce leaves (optional)

Cook pasta shells according to directions on the package. Drain; rinse with cold water.

In a large bowl, mix sour cream, mayonnaise, horseradish sauce, onion, seasoned salt and pepper. Stir in shrimp, cucumber, celery and pasta. Refrigerate until serving. If desired, serve on lettuce.

Yellow Squash & Watermelon Salad

6 cups cubed, seedless watermelon
2 medium yellow summer squash, chopped
2 medium zucchini, chopped
½ cup lemon juice
12 fresh mint leaves, torn
1 t salt
8 cups fresh arugula or baby spinach
1 cup crumbled feta cheese (4 oz.)

In a large bowl combine the first six ingredients. Just before serving, add arugula and feta cheese. Toss gently to combine.

Chicken Pasta Salad

1 pound bow-tie pasta
2 T olive oil
½ red onion, sliced into half moons
1 pound chicken breast; cut into thin strips
¾ cup green olives, pitted and halved
½ cup raisins
1 cup mayonnaise dressing (Hellman's with olive oil)
½ cup orange juice (or more to taste)

Cook pasta according to package instructions; set aside to cool. Add oil, chicken strips, onions, and raisins to a hot pan. Cook until chicken is cooked through and onions are softened. Set aside to cool. In a large bowl, combine Hellman's Dressing with orange juice and olive oil to create a dressing. Add cooked pasta, chicken, olives, raisins and onions to dressing and toss to coat.

Roasted Root Vegetable & Romaine Salad

2 medium fresh beets (about 12 oz.)
2 T olive oil
1¾ lbs. fresh carrots and turnips
4 medium shallots, peeled and quartered
6 T olive oil
2 T white wine vinegar

1 t Dijon mustard
1 t honey
1 clove garlic, minced
8 cups torn romaine
½ cup chopped pecans, roasted
¼ cup chopped fresh Italian flat-leaf parsley

Preheat oven to 375 degrees. Wash and peel beets; cut into 1 in. pieces. Place in a 2 quart baking dish. Toss with 1 T of olive oil. Season to taste with salt and pepper. Cover tightly with foil. Roast 30 minutes.

Place turnips, parsnips and carrots in a 15x10x1 inch baking pan. Add shallots. Toss with remaining 1 T olive oil. Season with salt, wine vinegar, thyme, mustard, honey, garlic and salt and pepper to taste. Shake well. Serve, in a large bowl and toss.

Remove foil, add beets and stir. Increase temperature to 425 degrees. Return beets to oven. Place pan with carrot mixture next to beets. Roast, uncovered, 30 to 40 minutes or until tender.

For dressing, in a screw top jar, combine 6 T olive oil, white wine vinegar, thyme, Dijon mustard, honey, garlic and salt and pepper to taste. To serve, in a large bowl, toss romaine and dressing.

Heirloom Tomato & Zucchini Salad

7 large heirloom tomatoes (about 2 ½ pounds) *
3 medium zucchini (halved lengthwise; sliced thin)
2 medium sweet yellow peppers, sliced thin
⅓ cup cider vinegar
3 T olive oil
1 T sugar
1½ t salt
1 T each minced fresh basil, parsley and tarragon
cut into wedges

In a large bowl, combine tomato wedges, zucchini, and peppers. In a small bowl, whisk vinegar, oil, sugar and salt until blended. Stir in herbs. Just before serving, drizzle dressing over salad. Toss gently to coat.

Mediterranean Grilled Potato Salad

¼ lb. ea. green and yellow wax beans, each split
2 lb. mixed baby red and gold potatoes
5 T extra virgin olive oil
2 T fresh lemon juice
1½ t Dijon mustard
2 T chopped fresh oregano leaves
½ t each of kosher salt and black pepper
¾ cup mixed, pitted black and green olives
½ cup mild feta cheese, crumbled

In a sauce pan over high heat, bring lightly salted water to a boil; add beans. Cook 4 minutes until crisp. With a slotted spoon, transfer beans to a bowl of ice water to cool. Drain; wrap in paper towels.

Add potatoes until tender (12-15 minutes). Drain, cool to room temperature.

In a large serving bowl, whisk 4 T oil, lemon juice, mustard, oregano, salt and pepper. Add cooked beans and olives to the bowl.

Halve potatoes. Line up potatoes cut side down on skewers. Heat a grill over medium high heat. Brush skewers with remaining oil. Grill 7 minutes, turning once or twice. Remove potatoes from skewers; add to salad bowl. Toss mixture to coat with dressing. Top with feta; serve warm.

Moroccan Couscous Salad

5 T extra-virgin olive oil
2 - (6 oz.) pkgs. pearl (Israeli) couscous
⅓ cup raisins and sun-dried tomatoes (diced)
1 onion (1 cup) diced
3 garlic cloves (chopped)
1½ t ground cumin
¾ pounds thin carrots, peeled & sliced (2 cups)

¾ lb. yellow summer squash; trimmed & diced
3 T sherry or red wine vinegar
2 T harissa
1 t kosher salt
1 cup cilantro leaves, coarsely chopped

Heat 1 T oil in a large saucepan over medium-high heat. Add couscous and cook 2 minutes, stirring until lightly toasted. Add 4 cups water; bring to a boil. Reduce heat to low, cover, and cook 10-12 minutes or until water is mostly absorbed. Stir in raisins and tomatoes; remove from heat. Let stand, covered, 5 minutes or until no liquid remains. Transfer couscous to a large bowl.

In a large skilled, heat 1 T oil over medium heat; add onion, garlic and cumin. Sauté 1 minute; add carrots and squash. Sauté vegetables 5 minutes. Add to couscous along with remaining 3 T oil, vinegar, harissa, and salt. Gently toss to combine and coat with dressing. Let cool and then stir in cilantro before serving.

Chilled Shrimp Pasta Salad

10 medium ears of sweet corn, husks removed
¼ cup olive oil
1 t salt
¾ t coarsely ground pepper
¾ t crushed red pepper flakes
2 large tomatoes, finely chopped
1 medium onion, thinly sliced
12 fresh basil leaves, sliced thin
1 cup zesty Italian salad dressing

Brush corn with oil. Grill corn, covered, over medium heat for 10-12 minutes or until lightly browned and tender, turning occasionally. Cool slightly.

Cut corn from cobs, transfer to a small bowl. Stir in salt, pepper, and pepper flakes. In a 2-quart glass bowl, layer a third of each of the following; corn, tomatoes, onion and basil. Repeat layers twice. Pour dressing over top; refrigerate before serving.

Caprese Orzo Salad

2 cups dry orzo pasta
2 balls fresh mozzarella cheese*
1 pint grape tomatoes, halved or quartered
6 to 9 fresh basil, washed & cut chiffonade style
2 to 3 extra virgin olive oil
Kosher salt and pepper
* diced into half-inch cubes

Cook the orzo pasta according to the directions on the package. Rinse immediately with cold water to stop the cooking process and refrigerate for 1 hour before mixing with other ingredients.

Just before serving, toss with fresh mozzarella, grape tomatoes, fresh basil and olive oil until well mixed. Add more oil if needed to lightly coat all ingredients. Season well with Kosher salt and pepper, starting with 1 t salt and 1 t pepper. Taste and add more seasoning as desired. Serve immediately.

Radicchio & Apple Salad with Parmesan Chips

6 oz. parmesan, finely grated, divided
2 T honey
½ small shallot, finely chopped
⅓ cup olive oil
3 T white wine vinegar
1 T Dijon mustard
Kosher salt and freshly ground pepper

2 medium heads of radicchio, leaves
  separated*
1 medium bunch arugula, tough stems
  removed
1 large Pink Lady apple, thinly sliced
Flaky sea salt (such as Maldon)
*torn in half if large

Preheat oven to 350 degrees. On a silicone mat-lined baking sheet, divide 4 oz. grated parmesan into 8 mounds. (Alternately line with parchment paper and coat with non-stick spray.) Press with your fingers to flatten. Bake until cheese is golden and melted, 6-8 minutes. Transfer baking sheet to a wire rack and let cool; break crisps into coarse pieces.

Heat honey in a small skillet over medium heat until warmed through. Whisk honey, shallot, oil, vinegar, and mustard in a large bowl; season with kosher salt and pepper.

Add radicchio, arugula, apple and remaining grated parmesan to vinaigrette; toss to coat. Season with sea salt and pepper. Serve topped with crisps.

Fennel, Celery & Pomegranate Salad

3 small fennel bulbs, thinly sliced
6 celery stalks, thinly sliced on a diagonal
1 medium shallot, thinly sliced into rings
½ cup fresh flat leaf parsley, very coarsely chopped
¼ cup celery leaves, very coarsely chopped*
½ cup pomegranate seeds, divided
⅓ cup fresh lime juice
⅓ cup olive oil
Kosher salt and freshly ground pepper
optional

Toss fennel, celery, shallot, parsley, celery leaves (if using) and half of pomegranate seeds in a large bowl. Drizzle with lime juice and oil and toss to coat; season with salt and pepper. Serve topped with remaining pomegranate seeds.

Orange Jicama Salad

1 T extra-light olive oil
1 heaping T brown sugar
1 T minced jalapeño pepper
1 T minced green onion
2 T chopped cilantro
2 very large oranges
10 oz. apple, peeled and diced

Combine oil, sugar, jalapeño, green onion and cilantro in a medium bowl. Mix well.

Peel oranges and cut orange slices away from membranes; add to bowl. Squeeze juice into bowl. Discard orange membranes.

Add jicama to bowl. Refrigerate up to one hour before serving. Toss well before serving.

Serves four

Venison & Wild Mushroom Salad

About one pound venison backstrap
4 T vegetable oil, divided
4 T butter, divided
1 pound wild mushrooms, stemmed and chopped
2 bunches kale, stems removed and chopped

2 cups chicken stock
¼ cup Parmigiano Reggiano cheese, grated
extra virgin olive oil for drizzling
salt and freshly ground pepper to taste

Preheat oven to 400 degrees. Rinse under cold water and pat dry with paper towels. Allow meat to come to room temperature, covered, about 30 minutes. Salt and pepper backstrap. Heat 3 T oil in oven-proof pan. When oil begins to smoke, add backstrap. Sear about 1½ minutes per side. Transfer pan to oven and roast 6 or 7 minutes. Remove from oven and let sit, tented with foil.

Heat 2 T butter and 1 T oil over medium high heat. Add mushrooms and cook about 4 minutes, stirring gently. Add kale in batches, as it wilts and cooks down; cook 5 minutes. Add chicken stock and remaining butter and continue to cook, uncovered, 2 minutes. Season with salt and pepper.

To serve, slice backstrap into medallions. Arrange kale-mushroom mixture on each plate and top with venison. Sprinkle grated cheese on each plate; drizzle with olive oil.

Pasta Salad (simple, but good)

SALAD INGREDIENTS
1 pkg. ring macaroni
1 pkg. coleslaw mix
Veggies of your choice, such as cucumbers, celery, onions peppers, peas, etc.

DRESSING INGREDIENTS
1½ cups salad dressing
½ cup sugar
1T vinegar
salt and pepper to taste

Cook macaroni, drain and cool. Combine macaroni, coleslaw mix and vegetables in a large bowl. Combine dressing ingredients. Pour over pasta mixture. Mix well and chill.

Wakame-Cucumber Salad

1 oz. dry wakame
½ cup distilled white vinegar
⅓ cup sugar
3 T Kosher salt
1 t black peppercorns
½ medium cucumber, sliced ¼ inch thick
¼ medium white radish, peeled and sliced thin

Soak wakame in a small bowl of cold water for 20 minutes. Drain and squeeze wakame gently to remove excess water. Cut into 1 to 2 inch pieces.

Meanwhile, bring vinegar, salt, sugar, peppercorns and 2 cups of water to a boil in a medium saucepan – whisking to dissolve sugar and salt, let cool.

Combine wakame, radish, cucumber, and pickling liquid in a medium bowl. Cover and chill at least 24 hours. Drain excess liquid just before serving.

Spicy Scallion & Onion Salad

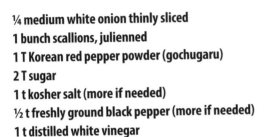

¼ medium white onion thinly sliced
1 bunch scallions, julienned
1 T Korean red pepper powder (gochugaru)
2 T sugar
1 t kosher salt (more if needed)
½ t freshly ground black pepper (more if needed)
1 t distilled white vinegar

Place onion and scallions in a medium bowl of cold water. Chill until scallions curl – at least 20 minutes.

Meanwhile, whisk gochugaru, sugar, 1 t salt, ½ t pepper, and 1T water in a medium bowl. Let sit, whisk occasionally, until sugar is dissolved and sauce looks shiny, about 10 minutes.

Drain onions and scallions and spin in a salad spinner or pat dry. Transfer to bowl with gochugaru sauce. Add vinegar and toss to coat; season with salt and pepper.

Onion and scallions can be soaked 1 day ahead.

Brussels Sprouts Salad

¼ of a day-old baguette (about a 6–8 inch piece)
3 T extra virgin olive oil (divided)
3 garlic cloves, divided
1 small red onion
4 t lemon juice

1 pound brussels sprouts (about 12)
½ cup flat leaf parsley, loosely packed
2 oz. shaved Parmesan
¼ t salt
Dash freshly ground pepper

Preheat oven to 375 degrees. Slice the baguette in half (lengthwise). Drizzle the cut sides with 1 t olive oil. Season with salt and pepper and bake until golden (about 10–12 minutes). Remove from oven and rub immediately with 1 cut clove of garlic. Once cool, tear into bite-size pieces and add to a large mixing bowl.

Peel and halve the onion, then slice. Peel and smash the two remaining garlic cloves. Heat a sauté pan over medium heat. Add 1 T of olive oil, then the garlic and onions. Season with salt and pepper and cook slowly over low heat until tender, 10–12 minutes. Remove the pan from heat, remove garlic cloves then add lemon juice and 3 T of olive oil to the onion mixture. Let rest in the sauté pan.

Trim the cut end of the sprouts lengthwise as thin as possible. Add to the mixing bowl. Pour the onion mixture over the top and toss well to combine. Finish with the parsley leaves and parmesan. Add salt, pepper and lemon juice to taste.

Serves four

Fruit Salad for a Crowd

SALAD
4 Golden Delicious apples, not peeled, diced
4 Red Delicious apples, not peeled, diced
2 cups green seedless grapes, halved
2 cups red seedless grapes, halved
1 - 20 oz. can pineapple chunks, drained
1 - 20 oz. can mandarin oranges, drained

DRESSING
1 - 3 oz. pkg. cream cheese, softened
½ cup sour cream
½ cup mayonnaise
½ cup sugar

Cut the pineapple and the cantaloupe into bite-sized pieces and put them in a large bowl. Peel the mangoes with potato peeler. Cut the fruit from the mango seeds and cut it into bite-sized pieces, adding it to the bowl. Wash the strawberries, grapes, and blueberries. Cut the strawberries into bite-sized pieces, and add all to the bowl. The amount of powdered sugar depends on how much fruit you have, how ripe your fruit is, and personal preference. Start by adding about 3 cups powdered sugar to the fruit bowl and stir to combine until the powdered sugar mixes with the juices from the fruits and no longer looks white. Do a taste test and add more powdered sugar if desired.

Oriental Salad

SALAD

1 small head of cabbage, shredded
4 green onions with half the tops chopped
1 pkg. Ramen noodles, crushed, uncooked
3 T sesame seeds
½ cup slivered almonds

DRESSING

½ cup olive oil
3 T white vinegar
3 T sugar
Flavor packet from noodles

Toast the sesame seeds and slivered almonds in a small amount of oil over medium heat. Set aside. Combine dressing ingredients. Mix together and pour over cabbage mixture. Salt to taste.

Roasted Beet Salad

3 medium beets, washed and trimmed
¼ cup extra virgin olive oil
2 T sherry vinegar
1 T honey
1 T minced red onions
½ T Dijon mustard
4 cups baby spinach
½ cup crumbled goat cheese
½ cup chopped walnuts

Preheat oven to 400 degrees. Wrap the beets in foil packets and roast in the oven until tender (about 1 hour). Open the foil packets and let cool. Once cool enough to handle, peel using a paper towel, then dice.

In a medium bowl, whisk together the olive oil, vinegar, honey, red onions and mustard. Add the beets and spinach to the dressing and toss to coat. Top with the goat cheese and walnuts.

Serves six

Tangy Cucumber Salad

Thinly slice 3 small cucumbers. Toss with 1 T of salt in a colander and let sit 15 minutes.

Mix cucumber with ½ small thinly sliced red onion, 3 T olive oil, and 3 T white wine vinegar. Season with salt and pepper and let sit 20 minutes.

Serves two to four as a side dish

Heirloom Tomato & Zucchini Salad

Divide 1 pound heirloom (large) tomatoes, cut into ¼ inch thick slices, 1 small zucchini cut into 1/8 inch thick rounds, evenly on four plates.

Sprinkle with ¼ T kosher salt and ¼ T freshly ground black pepper.

Combine 2 T finely chopped fresh chives, 1 T olive oil, 1 T red wine vinegar, and 1 T sugar in a bowl, stirring with a whisk. Drizzle vinegar mixture evenly over salads.

Serves four

Macaroni Salad

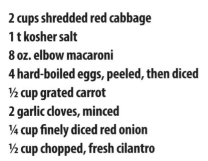

2 cups shredded red cabbage
1 t kosher salt
8 oz. elbow macaroni
4 hard-boiled eggs, peeled, then diced
½ cup grated carrot
2 garlic cloves, minced
¼ cup finely diced red onion
½ cup chopped, fresh cilantro

½ cup diced sweet cucumber pickles
¼ cup mayonnaise
1 T fresh lime juice
1 T prepared yellow mustard
1 canned chipotle chili in adobo sauce, diced
¼ t cumin

Put cabbage in a strainer and then place strainer in a bowl. Toss cabbage with salt and refrigerate 1 hour. This step will drain cabbage of its excess water and keep it crisp in the salad.

Cook macaroni according to the directions on the package, drain, rinse, and refrigerate for 1 hour.

One hour later, take cabbage from the strainer and place in a large mixing bowl. Add eggs, carrot, garlic, red onion, cilantro, pickles and macaroni.

Whisk together mayonnaise, lime juice, mustard, chipotle chili and cumin. Spoon dressing over salad and stir. Taste and adjust seasonings. Will taste better if refrigerated.

Quick Waldorf Chicken Salad

1 cup apples, cut into bite-size pieces
1 chicken breast, cooked and cut up
½ cup raisins
¼ cup walnuts
½ cup Miracle Whip
Sweetener and milk or cream

Whip Miracle Whip with small amount of sweetener and milk or cream. Mix with rest of ingredients.

Salad Featuring Sweet Potatoes

4 large sweet potatoes
6 T olive oil, divided
½ small red onion, sliced thin
½ cup frozen edamame, shelled and thawed
3 stalks of celery, thinly sliced
¼ cup fresh parsley, chopped
1 T fresh chives, minced
2 T lemon juice
1 T Dijon mustard
Salt and pepper to taste

Peel sweet potatoes and cut into 1 inch cubes. Heat a large, heavy skillet over medium high heat; add 1 T olive oil. Arrange half of potatoes in skillet in a single layer. Reduce heat to medium. Cook potatoes, covered, 4 to 5 minutes. Stir after 2 minutes. Transfer potatoes to a plate. Repeat process with 1 T olive oil and remaining potatoes.

Combine onion and next 4 ingredients in a bowl. Add potatoes to onion mixture; set aside.

Whisk together lemon juice, mustard, and olive oil in a bowl; drizzle over potatoes and toss. Season with salt and pepper. Serve immediately.

Bean & Pork Salad, Southwest Version

1 cup cooked pork, cubed
½ medium sweet red pepper, chopped
¾ cup frozen corn, thawed
½ cup canned kidney beans, rinsed & drained
¼ cup chopped green onions
2 T balsamic vinegar
1 T water
1 T olive oil
1 garlic clove, minced
¼ t salt
¼ t pepper
¼ t hot pepper sauce
lettuce leaves

In a bowl, combine the first 5 ingredients. In another bowl, whisk the vinegar, water, oil, garlic, salt, pepper and hot pepper sauce. Pour over pork mixture and toss to coat.

Cover and refrigerate at least 30 minutes. Serve on plates lined with lettuce.

Serves two

Tossed Cauliflower Salad

1 cup fresh cauliflowerets
¼ cup thinly sliced red onion, quartered
2 T sliced stuffed olives
2 T canola oil
1 T tarragon vinegar
¼ T sugar
1/8 t salt
Dash paprika
2 cups torn leaf lettuce
2 T crumbled blue cheese

In a small bowl, combine cauliflower, onions and olives. In another bowl, whisk the oil, vinegar, sugar, salt and paprika. Drizzle over cauliflower mixture and toss to coat. Refrigerate 1 hour or until chilled. Just before serving, add the lettuce and blue cheese; toss.

Serves two

Salad Made with Grilled Sirloin

5 T plus 1 t olive oil, divided
4 T red wine vinegar, divided
½ pound boneless beef sirloin steak
½ medium red onion, sliced and cut into rings
½ medium green pepper, julienned

4 cups torn mixed salad greens
½ cup fresh raspberries
¼ T salt
¼ T pepper

In a large reusable plastic bag, combine 2 T oil and 1 T vinegar; add the steak; seal bag and turn to coat. Refrigerate for one hour.

Place onion and green pepper on a double thickness of heavy-duty foil (about 12 in. square). Fold foil around the vegetable and seal tightly. Cut about 6-one inch slots in top of packet. Set aside.

Coat grill rack with non-stick cooking spray before starting the grill. Drain and discard marinade. Grill steak covered over medium heat for 6-8 minutes on each side. Grill vegetable packet for 8-10 minutes, turning once.

Let steak stand 5 minutes. Meanwhile, in a bowl, combine the salad greens, raspberries and grilled vegetables. In a bowl, whisk the salt, pepper and remaining oil and vinegar. Pour over salad and toss to coat, slice steak across grain, arrange over salad.

Serves two

Salad From Tomatoes & Eggplant

4 small eggplants
Kosher salt
Canola oil for frying
8 large red pearl onions, peeled
1 t cumin seed
½ small red onion, thinly sliced
¾ cup white vinegar
1½ T red chili powder

1 t ground fennel
1 t ground turmeric
5 canned whole peeled tomatoes,
   crushed by hand
4 small green Thai chiles, halved
   lengthwise, stems on
1 stick cinnamon

Peel eggplants and quarter them lengthwise, leaving stems attached. Toss eggplant and salt in a colander set over a bowl. Drain 1 hour, then pat dry using paper towels.

Heat 2 inches of oil in a 6 quart saucepan to 375 degrees. In batches, fry eggplant until golden, 1 to 2 minutes. Use a slotted spoon to transfer eggplant to paper towels. Fry pearl onions until golden, 3 to 4 minutes; transfer to paper towels to drain.

Discard all but ½ cup oil; return to medium high heat. Cook cumin seeds and sliced onion until onion is golden. Add remaining ingredients plus ¾ cup water; boil. Reduce heat to medium; cook until tomatoes are broken down. Add eggplant and pearl onions; Add eggplant and pearl onions; cook until coated in sauce (2-3 minutes).

Serves four

Fruit Salad with Yogurt

½ cup reduced fat vanilla yogurt
1½ T honey
½ T lemon juice
1 cup mandarin oranges, drained
½ small apple, chopped
4 strawberries, sliced
1 plum, sliced
2 T chopped pecans, toasted

In a small bowl combine the yogurt, honey and lemon juice. Add fruit; toss gently to coat.

Cover and refrigerate until serving. Sprinkle with pecans.

Serves two

Creamy Mushroom & Fresh Herb Salad

½ oz. dried porcini mushrooms
1 pound whole wheat penne
1 T butter, divided
5 oz. shiitake, sliced and divided
8 oz. sliced crimini mushrooms, divided
⅓ cup finely chopped shallots
2 garlic cloves, minced

2 T minced fresh thyme
½ T salt
¼ T freshly ground black pepper
½ cup dry white wine
⅓ cup heavy whipping cream
⅓ cup fresh Parmigiano-Reggiano cheese
3 T freshly chopped parsley, plus garnish

Soak dried mushrooms in ½ cup of hot water until softened, about 20 minutes, swishing around occasionally. Remove the mushrooms, straining the liquid through a paper coffee filter and reserve the liquid. Slice the mushrooms thinly; set aside.

Cook pasta according to pkg. directions. Reserve ½ cup of the pasta water before draining. While the pasta is cooking, heat half of the butter and half of the oil in a large nonstick skillet over medium-high heat. Add half of the shiitake and crimini mushrooms and sauté until lightly browned. Transfer to a plate and repeat with the remaining butter, oil, and mushrooms to a plate and reduce heat to minimum. Add the shallots and sauté for a minute. Add the garlic, thyme, salt and pepper and continue to sauté for another minute. Add both the reserved cooked fresh mushrooms and soaked dry mushrooms and wine; cook 2 minutes stirring occasionally. Add the cream and cook another 2 minutes. Add the cooked pasta, cheese and parsley, tossing gently. Divide among 6 warm serving plates. Garnish with minced parsley and serve immediately.

Herb Salad with Fennel & Horseradish

2 T coarsely chopped pistachios
1 T fennel seeds
1 T plus ¼ cup olive oil
Kosher salt
1 small fennel bulb, thinly sliced-lengthwise
4 cups torn butter lettuce
1½ cups fresh parsley leaves with

tender stems
½ cup fresh tarragon leaves (torn if large)
3 T chopped fresh chives
1 T finely grated lemon zest
2 T fresh lemon juice
2 T grated peeled horseradish
freshly ground black pepper

Toss pistachios, fennel seeds, and 1 T oil in a small skillet over medium heat and cook, stirring occasionally, until fragrant (about 3 minutes). Season with salt. Transfer to a small bowel; let cool.

Toss fennel, parsley, lettuce, tarragon, chives, lemon zest, and horseradish in a large bowl; add lemon juice; season with salt and pepper and toss to coat.

Add remaining ¼ cup of oil and toss to coat, then add half of the pistachio mixture and toss enough to combine. Season with salt, pepper, and more lemon juice.

Serve salad topped with remaining pistachio mixture.

Grape-Watermelon Salad

2 cups cubed, seeded watermelon
2 cups seedless red grapes
4 T white grape juice
1 T finely chopped fresh tarragon
1 T honey

In a small bowl, combine grapes and watermelon. In another bowl, whisk the grape juice, tarragon and honey. Pour over fruit and toss to coat. Serve immediately.

Serves four

Farro Salad With Cherry Tomato, Onion & Almonds

9 oz. uncooked pearled farro
1½ cups sliced, halved cucumbers
1½ cups quartered cherry tomatoes
½ cup fresh flat leaf parsley
¼ cup multipurpose vinaigrette
1 T mascarpone cheese
¼ cup lightly salted smoked almonds, chopped

Cook farro according to package directions, omitting salt; drain in a colander. Rinse with cold water for 30 seconds; drain. Cook to room temperature.

Combine cooked farro, cucumber, tomatoes, onion and parsley in a large bowl.

Combine vinaigrette and mascarpone in a bowl, stirring with a whisk. Pour over farro mixture, tossing to combine. Top with almonds.

Shaved Zucchini & Parsley Salad

3 medium zucchini
¼ cup chopped fresh flat leaf parsley
¼ cup thinly, vertically sliced red onion
¼ cup multipurpose vinaigrette
3 T crumbled feta cheese

Slice zucchini into thin ribbons using a vegetable peeler; toss with parsley, onion, and vinaigrette. Sprinkle with cheese.

Salad in a Jar

2 T extra virgin olive oil, divided
¾ cup uncooked quinoa
1 cup unsalted chicken stock
½ T salt, divided
2 T fresh lemon juice
¼ T freshly ground black pepper
Dash of sugar

1 garlic clove, minced
2 cups baby arugula leaves
1 cup diced cucumber
½ cup diced red onion
1 cup grape tomatoes, halved
¾ cup chopped fresh flat-leaf parsley

Heat a small saucepan over medium high heat. Add 1 T oil; swirl to coat. Add quinoa; cook 2 minutes or until lightly toasted, stirring frequently. Gradually stir in stock; bring to a boil. Cover, reduce heat and simmer 13 minutes. Remove from heat; stir in ¼ T salt. Cool the quinoa to room temperature.

Combine remaining 5 t oil, remaining ¼ T salt, juice, pepper, sugar and garlic in a small bowl; stirring with a whisk.

Place about 1T dressing in each of 4 pint-size jars with lids. Layer ½ cup arugula, ¼ of quinoa mixture, ¼ cup cucumber, 2 T onion, ¼ cup tomato, and 3 T parsley in each jar. Close lid; refrigerate up to 24 hours. Shake before serving.

Serves four

Coleslaw

2 T rice wine vinegar
2 T vegetable oil
2 T honey
2 T dark sesame oil
¼ t salt
¼ t freshly ground black pepper
5 cups Napa cabbage or Chinese cabbage, thinly sliced
1 carrot, peeled and grated
½ cup red bell pepper, seeded and thinly sliced
⅓ cup cilantro, finely chopped

In a large bowl, combine the rice wine, vegetable oil, honey, sesame oil, ¼ T salt, ¼ T pepper.

Whisk it together and add the cabbage, carrot, bell pepper, and cilantro.

Toss to coat and set aside. Optional: refrigerate.

Cobb Salad Pizza

1- (11 oz.) can refrigerated thin-crust
   pizza dough
Cooking spray
¼ cup crumbled blue cheese, divided
1 T extra virgin olive oil
1 T white wine vinegar
½ t Dijon mustard
¼ t black pepper, divided

2 slices smoked bacon
8 oz. skinless, boneless chicken
   breast cutlets
½ cup quartered cherry tomatoes
2 T chopped red onion
2 cups mixed baby greens (lightly packed)
½ cup diced peeled avocado

Preheat oven to 425 degrees. Unroll dough on a baking sheet coated with cooking spray, pat dough into a 14x12 inch rectangle. Lightly coat dough with cooking spray. Bake at 425 degrees for 8 minutes. Remove from oven, sprinkle evenly with 2 T cheese.

Combine oil, vinegar, mustard, and ⅛ t pepper in a bowl (use whisk).

Cook bacon in a large non-stick skillet over medium heat until crisp. Remove bacon and crumble into oil mixture. Wipe pan clean with paper towels. Heat pan with medium heat. Coat pan with cooking spray. Sprinkle chicken with remaining ⅛ t pepper. Add chicken to pan; cook 4 minutes on each side. Remove chicken and chop into ½ inch pieces.

Add chicken, tomatoes, and onion to oil mixture; toss. Add greens, toss. Top crust evenly with chicken mixture, avocado and cheese. Cut into 8 pieces.

Chopped Romaine Salad

1 T olive oil
1 T red wine vinegar
½ T chopped fresh oregano
¼ t grated lemon rind
¼ t kosher salt
Large bowl

Combine 1 T olive oil, 1 T red wine vinegar, ½ t chopped fresh oregano, ¼ t rated lemon rind, and ¼ t Kosher salt in a large bowl, stirring with a whisk.

Add 3 cups chopped romaine lettuce, 1 cup quartered cherry tomatoes, and ¼ cup vertically sliced red onion. Toss gently to coat.

Ribbon Zucchini Salad

1 lb. small yellow and green zucchini
⅔ cup raw almonds
⅓ cup extra virgin olive oil
1 T grated lemon zest
2 oz. dry Jack cheese, grated
½ t sea salt
Freshly ground pepper to taste
12 mint leaves

Wash, top, and shave zucchini into ribbons using a vegetable peeler. Heat oven to 350 degrees. Bake the almonds 8 minutes. Remove, let cool, crush gently.

Combine all ingredients in a large bowl and toss gently. Serve.

Serves four

Caramelized Veggie Lentil Salad

2½ fennel bulbs, cored, quartered, sliced thin.
1 lb. carrots, peeled and chopped
3 T butter, melted
4 cups reduced-sodium chicken broth
2 cups dried French green lentils
6 cloves of garlic, minced
2 bay leaves

½ cup extra virgin olive oil
3 T country Dijon-style mustard
1 T balsamic vinegar
1 T honey, warmed
2 cups Italian parsley leaves, finely chopped
2 large shallots, finely chopped
6 large sage leaves, finely chopped

Preheat oven to 425 degrees. In a shallow baking pan, toss fennel and carrots with melted butter; season generously with salt and pepper. Roast 30 minutes, stirring occasionally until tender.

In a 4 quart pot, combine chicken broth, lentils, garlic and bay leaves. Bring to boiling; reduce heat, simmer uncovered 20 to 25 minutes – drain. Discard bay leaves. Stir in ½ T salt.

In a large bowl, whisk together olive oil, mustard, balsamic vinegar and honey. Add lentils, parsley, shallots, and sage. Stir in caramelized vegetables. Refrigerate up to 4 days. Serve cold or at room temperature. Makes 12 cups.

Fall Flavored Salad

SALAD INGREDIENTS
1 pkg. mixed greens
¼ cup dried figs quartered
¼ cup dried apricots, sliced
¼ cup dried cranberries
¼ cup dried pineapple chunks
¼ cup smoked Gouda, shredded
⅓ cup toasted pine nuts
¼ cup white cranberry vinaigrette

VINAIGRETTE INGREDIENTS
½ cup white cherry juice
½ cup extra virgin olive oil
1 t salt
1 t honey
2 t Dijon mustard
¼ cup white wine vinegar

Prepare the vinaigrette first. Use a whisk or food processor to mix all vinaigrette ingredients together, except the olive oil, until well combined. Continue to whisk or blend while adding the oil in a slow steady stream until the oil is fully incorporated.

Toss the greens with the vinaigrette until leaves are evenly coated. Refrigerate any remaining vinaigrette for up to 1 week.

Arrange the leaves on serving plates; then top them first with the dried fruit, then the shredded cheese, finishing with the toasted pine nuts.

Citrus & Smoked Almond Salad

¼ **cup orange juice**
3 **T lemon juice**
¼ **cup extra virgin olive oil**
½ **t salt**
¼ **t cracked black pepper**
10 **oz. mixed greens**
1 **cup orange slices**
1 **cup grapefruit slices**
¾ **cup pomegranate seeds**
¾ **cup chopped, smoked almonds**

In a large bowl, whisk together orange juice, lemon juice, olive oil, salt, and black pepper.

Add mixed greens, orange slices, grapefruit slices, pomegranate seeds, and chopped smoked almonds. Toss to coat. Makes 16 1-cup servings.

Roasted Butternut Squash Salad

¼ cup sherry vinegar
¼ cup walnut oil
2 t minced garlic
2 t each fresh rosemary and sage
½ t salt
¼ t cracked black pepper
10 oz. mixed greens
4 cups roasted butternut squash
1½ cups Manchego cheese
1/3 cup salted, roasted pepitas

In a large bowl whisk together the vinegar, walnut oil, garlic, and 2 t each roasemary, sage, salt and black pepper.

Add mixed greens, butternut squash, Manchego cheese, and roasted pepitas. Toss to coat.

Makes twelve one-cup servings

Shaved Fennel & Celery Salad

6 T lemon juice
⅓ cup extra virgin olive oil
2 T minced shallot
½ t sugar
½ t salt
¼ t black pepper
10 oz. mixed greens
2 cups thinly sliced celery
1 cup shaved parmesan cheese

In a large bowl, whisk together lemon, olive oil, minced shallot, sugar, salt, black pepper, mixed greens, celery, fennel, and 1 cup shaved parmesan cheese. Toss to coat.

Makes twelve one-cup servings

Avocado & Roasted Carrot Salad

½ avocado, mashed until smooth
⅓ cup red wine vinegar
¼ cup extra virgin olive oil
½ t kosher salt
½ t dried oregano
¼ t cracked black pepper
10 oz. mixed greens
3 sliced avocados
3 cups roasted carrot strips
¾ cup sliced green onions
1½ cups queso fresco

In a large bowl, mash the avocado until smooth. Whisk in the red wine vinegar, extra virgin olive oil, kosher salt, dried oregano, and cracked black pepper. Add mixed greens, avocados, carrot strips, and green onions, and queso fresco.

Makes twelve one-cup servings

Brussels Sprout Salad with Parmesan & Walnuts

1 pound brussels sprouts, thinly sliced
1 apple, shredded
1 cup toasted walnuts, chopped
¼ cup grated parmigiano
¼ cup extra-virgin olive oil
¼ cup lemon juice
½ t coarse salt
Freshly ground black pepper

Place Brussels sprouts and apple in a bowl and toss lightly to separate the layers of sprouts. Add walnuts and cheese. Combine olive oil, lemon juice, salt, and pepper, whisking well. Drizzle over sprout mixture. Toss well. Serve immediately.

Serves eight

Simple Salad with Parmesan

2½ T fresh lemon juice
2 T canola mayonnaise
1 T extra virgin olive oil
½ t sugar
½ t ground black pepper
6 cups melted baby greens
½ cup halved cherry tomatoes
1 oz. shaved Parmesan cheese

Combine lemon juice, mayonnaise, olive oil, sugar, and black pepper, stirring with a whisk.
Add baby greens; toss to coat. Sprinkle with halved cherry tomatoes and Parmesan cheese.

Serves four

Carrot - Fennel Salad

3 T olive oil
3 T white wine vinegar
2 T Dijon mustard
½ t salt
¾ t black pepper
1 large fennel bulb
1 pound carrots, shaved with vegetable peeler
½ cup pistachios, shelled but unsalted
½ cup fresh parsley, chopped

In a large bowl, whisk oil, vinegar, mustard, salt and pepper.

Toss in fennel, carrots, pistachios and parsley. Season with remaining ¼ t salt.

Zesty Summer Salad

Kernels from 6 ears of fresh corn
4 handsful baby spinach, chopped
1 red bell pepper, chopped
½ cup olive oil
2 limes, juiced
½ t paprika
Salt and pepper to taste
1½ t ground cumin
Cilantro (as a garnish)
Optional: 1 beet chopped for color

Combine zest from 1 line, lime juice, oil and seasoning. Add rest of the ingredients in a bowl. Toss the dressing and let it sit 15 minutes; mix.

Serves four or five

Tomato & Peach Salad with Almonds

1 T canola oil
1 t white wine vinegar
1 t honey
2 medium tomatoes cut into ¼ inch slices
1 medium peach, pitted and sliced
2 T sliced toasted almonds
1 T fresh mint leaves
⅛ T kosher salt
⅛ T black pepper

Combine oil, vinegar and honey in a small bowl. Divide tomato and peach slices evenly among 4 plates.

Top with almonds, mint, salt and pepper. Drizzle with honey mixture.

Serves four

Caesar Breadcrumb Salad

4 t olive oil
1 garlic clove, minced
¼ t anchovy paste
½ cup fresh bread crumbs
⅛ t kosher salt
2 cups arugula
1½ t balsamic
2 tomatoes, sliced

Heat olive oil, garlic clove, and anchovy paste in a skillet over medium heat 1 minute. Add bread crumbs. Cook 1½ minutes. Combine oil, arugula, and balsamic.

Top with sliced tomatoes, kosher salt, and breadcrumbs.

Serves four

Halloumi Cheese & Oregano Salad

2 t canola oil
1.5 ounces halloumi cheese, thinly sliced
2 tomatoes, sliced
1 T fresh lemon juice
1 T fresh oregano leaves
⅛ t kosher salt
⅛ t black pepper

Heat canola oil in a non-stick skillet over medium heat. Add halloumi cheese. Cook 2 minutes on each side.

Top sliced tomatoes with halloumi cheese, lemon juice, oregano leaves, kosher salt and black pepper.

Wild Rice Salad

1½ cups uncooked wild rice
2½ cups uncooked brown rice
4 cloves garlic, chopped fine
1 t dried marjoram
1 t dried basil
1 t Dijon mustard
Salt and pepper

¾ cup olive oil
¼ cup red wine vinegar
½ cup pecans, coarsely chopped
1 bunch green onions, sliced diagonally
½ cup dried cranberries
4 cups spinach, sliced into a wide
   chiffonade

Cook wild rice and brown rice according to the directions on their packages.

DIRECTIONS FOR PREPARING DRESSING

Whisk together garlic, marjoram, basil, and mustard, olive oil, red wine vinegar, and salt and pepper to taste. Pour the dressing over the rice when rice is at room temperature. Store refrigerated overnight covered with plastic wrap.

When served, add pecans, green onions, cranberries, and spinach. Season with salt and pepper to taste.

Grilled Lemon-Chicken with Tomato Salad

1 t grated lemon rind
4 T fresh lemon juice, divided
3 T extra-virgin olive oil
4 (6 oz.) skinless, boneless, chicken breasts
½ t kosher salt, divided
½ t black pepper, divided
2 cups baby heirloom tomatoes
⅓ cup feta cheese, crumbled
Cooking spray

Combine rind, 2 T juice and 1 T oil in a large zip-top plastic bag. Add chicken; turn to coat. Let stand 8 minutes.

Combine remaining 2 T juice, remaining 2 T oil, ¼ t salt and ¼ t pepper in a bowl. Stir in tomatoes and feta cheese.

Heat a grill plan over medium high heat. Coat pan with cooking spray. Sprinkle chicken with remaining ¼ t pepper; grill 5 minutes on each side until done.
Top chicken with tomato mixture.

Serves four

Celery Caesar Salad

2 slices country style bread, torn into
   bite-size pieces
2 T olive oil
Kosher salt
1 large egg yolk
1 anchovy fillet, chopped
1 small garlic clove, chopped
1 T fresh lemon juice
1½ t white wine vinegar

½ t Dijon mustard
¼ cup vegetable oil
Freshly ground black pepper
⅓ cup Parmesan, grated and shaved
2 romaine hearts, leaves separated
8 celery stalk hearts, leaves separated
¼ large celery root, peeled & cut into
   match sticks

Preheat oven to 400 degrees. Toss bread with olive oil on a rimmed baking sheet. Season with salt. Toast, tossing halfway through. (5-10 minutes.) Let croutons cool.

Blend egg yolk, anchovy, garlic, lemon juice, vinegar, and mustard in a blender until smooth. With motor running, gradually drizzle in vegetable oil, blending until thickened. Dressing should be pourable.

Transfer to a bowl large enough to hold salad; season with salt and pepper. Mix in grated parmesan. Add romaine, celery stalks and leaves, and celery root; toss to coat.

Serve salad topped with croutons and shaved parmesan.

Fish & Peach Salad with Lemon-Mint Vinaigrette

3 T extra-virgin olive oil, divided
4 – 6oz. fish fillets
½ t kosher salt, divided
½ t freshly ground pepper, divided
2 T chopped fresh mint
2 T fresh lemon juice

1 t maple syrup
6 cups baby spinach leaves
2 medium peaches, halved and sliced
¼ cup toasted sliced almonds
½ English cucumber, halved lengthwise

Heat a non-stick skillet over medium-high heat. Add 1 T oil; swirl to coat. Sprinkle fish evenly with ¼ t salt and ¼ t pepper. Add fish to pan; cook 3 minutes on each side or until fish flakes easily when tested with a fork.

Combine remaining ¼ salt and remaining ¼ t pepper, remaining 2 T oil, mint, juice, and syrup in a large bowl, stirring with a whisk. Add spinach, peaches, mixture divided among 4 plates; top with fish. Sprinkle with almonds.

Serves four

Cabbage & Apple Salad

½ t caraway seeds
½ small head green cabbage, core removed; sliced thin
1 small, green apple, cut into matchsticks
1 cup torn kale leaves
2 T fresh lemon juice
2 T olive oil
Kosher salt, freshly ground pepper

Toast caraway seeds in a dry small skillet over medium heat, tossing constantly until fragrant, about 1 minute. Let cool.

Toss apple, cabbage, kale, and caraway seeds with lemon juice and oil in a large bowl; season with salt and pepper.

Avocado & Onion Salad

2 sliced tomatoes
1 sliced, peeled avocado
¼ cup white onion, sliced vertically
1 T chopped, fresh cilantro
1 T fresh lemon juice
¼ t chipotle chili powder
¼ t kosher salt
⅛ t freshly ground black pepper

Arrange sliced tomatoes and avocado on a platter; top evenly with sliced white onion, cilantro, lemon juice, chipotle chili powder, kosher salt and freshly ground black pepper.

Serves four

Chicken or Turkey & Wild Rice Salad with Orange Honey Vinaigrette

INGREDIENTS FOR THE DRESSING
Zest of one orange
Juice of one orange
⅓ cup extra virgin olive oil
1 large shallot, chopped
2 t honey
salt and freshly ground pepper

INGREDIENTS FOR THE SALAD
4 cups cooked wild rice
2 celery ribs with leaves, chopped
1 small red pepper, seeded and chopped
6 green onions, thinly sliced diagonally
2½ cups diced turkey or chicken meat
1 cup dried cranberries
6 cups winter spinach or dark greens
for serving
1 cup pecans, toasted

To make the dressing, in a large bowl, whisk together the orange zest and juice, oil, shallot and honey. Season with salt and pepper.

To assemble the salad, combine celery, wild rice, red pepper, green onions, turkey or chicken, and cranberries with the dressing.

Serve the salad on a bed of spinach or dark greens and scatter pecans on top.

Kid's Chef Salad

1 bag fresh Express Veggie Spring Mix
2 pieces of your child's favorite lunch meat
2 pieces of your child's favorite cheese
1 hard-boiled egg, chopped
2 slices turkey bacon, chopped
Child's favorite dressing (ranch or Italian)

Have child tear bite-size pieces of lunch meat and cheese.

While child is doing this, place egg in a sauce pan with enough water to cover it. Heat over high heat to just boiling. Remove from burner and cover pan. Let stand about 12 minutes. When done, transfer egg to an ice bath.

When egg is cooled, take the shell off and chop egg; set aside.

Cook turkey bacon according to instructions on the package. When cooked, cool, then chop into small pieces.

In a bowl, combine all ingredients except for dressing. Transfer to a reusable dish with dressing on the side.

Have child drizzle dressing on the salad.

Bok Choy, Radish & Orange Salad with Cilantro

2 oranges
1 garlic clove
2 T raspberry vinegar
1 large pinch of cayenne
2 to 3 t extra virgin olive oil
1 large or 2 small heads bok choy, thinly sliced
8 small radishes, cut into thin rounds
5 green onions, white and green parts sliced thin
⅓ cup fresh cilantro leaves
2 t mint leaves, thinly chopped

Grate 1 t of zest from an orange and reserve. Peel oranges, making sure to remove all the bitter white pith, and slice them into wheels.

In a small bowl, mash the garlic and then work in cayenne and vinegar. Whisk in olive oil and orange zest.

Place bok choy on a large serving platter or individual plates. Arrange radishes on top of bok choy. Drizzle with dressing, and scatter green onions, cilantro and mint on top.

Summer Garden Salad

1 bag mixed greens
5 radishes, washed and thinly sliced
2 lg. carrots, peeled and cut into julienne strips
1 bulb fennel, thinly sliced
¼ cup balsamic vinaigrette

In a large bowl, toss the greens with the vinaigrette until lightly coated, saving some dressing until later.

Arrange the vegetable colorfully around the salad, layering as desired. Drizzle the remaining vinaigrette over the vegetables and top of salad to garnish.

Creamy Sweet Potato Salad

4 medium sweet potatoes, peeled and chopped
2 T olive oil
2 T red wine vinegar
4 hard-boiled eggs, chopped
¼ cup peppadew peppers
½ cup sliced green onions
¼ cup chopped fresh dill
⅓ cup mayonnaise
⅓ cup plain Greek yogurt

Preheat oven to 400 degrees. In a large bowl combine potatoes and oil. Season with salt and pepper. Transfer to a shallow baking pan. Roast 15 minutes or until tender. Remove from oven.

Return potatoes to a large bowl. Drizzle with vinegar; stir to coat. Cool completely. Add eggs, peppers, green onions, and dill. In a small bowl combine mayonnaise and yogurt. Pour over potato mixture; toss. Season to taste with salt and pepper. Serve immediately. Makes 6 cups or 8-10 servings.

Make ahead: Assemble salad, preparing dressing separately. Cover; refrigerate up to 24 hours. Toss salad with dressing before serving.

Corn & Peach Salad

4 ears fresh corn, shucked
1 cup chopped fresh peaches
6 to 8 medium radishes, thinly sliced
¼ cup chopped fresh mint leaves
2 T olive oil
1 t cider vinegar

Remove husks from ears of corn. Scrub with a stiff brush to remove silks; rinse. Cut kernels from cobb (about 2 cups).

In a bowl, combine corn, peaches, radishes and mint. For dressing, add oil, and vinegar; toss to coat. Season to taste with salt and pepper. Serve immediately.

MAKE AHEAD
Assemble salad without mixing. Cover; refrigerate up to 24 hours. Add oil and vinegar.
Toss before serving.

Makes four cups or eight to ten servings

Radicchio Caesar Salad

1 9 oz. pkg. refrigerated 3 cheese tortellini
8 oz. sugar snap peas, trimmed and halved*
1 cup fresh mint leaves
1 cup fresh basil leaves
3 T sliced almonds, toasted
2 T grated Parmesan cheese
1 t grated lemon rind

¼ t freshly ground black pepper
⅛ t Kosher salt
1 garlic clove, minced
3 T olive oil
1 T fresh lemon juice
*halved diagonally, about 1 ½ cups

Cook tortellini according to pkg. directions, omitting salt and fat. Add snap peas to pan during last 3 minutes of cooking (cook 3 minutes). Drain.

Place mint and next 7 ingredients (through garlic) in a mini food processor; process until finely chopped, scraping sides of bowl once. Combine oil and juice in a small bowl, stirring with a whisk. With processor on, slowly pour oil mixture through food chute; process until well blended. Combine tortellini mixture and mint mixture, toss gently to coat.

Serves four

Tarragon-Tomato Salad

1 minced shallot
1 T fresh tarragon
1½ T white wine vinegar
¼ t kosher salt
1/8 t freshly ground black pepper
3 T olive oil
4 medium ripe tomatoes, sliced

Combine shallot, tarragon, white wine vinegar, kosher salt, and black pepper in a jar. Let stand 10 minutes. Add olive oil; cover jar tightly and shake.

Arrange sliced tomatoes on a platter; drizzle with dressing.

Serves four

Cucumber, Black Olive & Mint Salad

2 cups thinly sliced cucumbers
¼ cup chopped, pitted black olives
3 T chopped, fresh mint
2 T fresh lemon juice
1 T olive oil
½ t freshly ground black pepper

Combine sliced cucumbers, chopped olives, chopped mint, lemon juice, olive oil, and black pepper.

Serves four

Arugula Fennel Salad

¼ cup white balsamic vinegar
¼ cup olive oil
1 clove garlic, minced
1 bulb fennel, trimmed and cored
3 cups arugula
1 cup cubed pineapple
½ cup golden raisins

In a large bowl, whisk together vinegar, oil, garlic, salt and pepper. Using a mandolin, slice fennel into a bowl. Add arugula, raisins, and pineapple; toss gently to combine.

Serves eight

Chopped Salad with Chive Vinaigrette

2 T fresh lemon juice
1 T minced fresh chives
1 t sugar
3/8 t kosher salt
¼ t freshly ground black pepper
3 T olive oil
2 chopped romaine hearts
1 diced cucumber
1 diced celery stalk

Combine lemon juice, chives, sugar, salt, and pepper. Whisk in the olive oil.

Toss with romaine hearts, cucumber, and diced celery stalk.

Serves four

Herb Salad with Mustard Vinaigrette

1 t red wine vinegar
1 t fresh orange juice
½ t whole grain mustard
¼ t salt
2 T olive oil
5 oz. pkg. herb salad

Combine red wine vinegar, orange juice, mustard, and salt; whisk in olive oil.

Pour over package of herb salad; toss to coat.

Serves four

Shaved Asparagus Salad with Manchego & Almonds

1½ T extra virgin olive oil
2 t sherry vinegar
1½ t walnut oil
1 t minced fresh garlic
¼ t fresh ground black pepper
1 pound large asparagus

1 t chopped fresh leaf parsley
8 cups of water
2 T white vinegar
4 large eggs
2 T Slivered almonds, toasted
1 oz. Manchego cheese, shaved (¼ cup)

Combine first 6 ingredients in a large bowl, stirring with a whisk. Using a shard peeler, thinly peel asparagus to equal 3 cups asparagus ribbons. Add asparagus and parsley to bowl; toss gently to coat.

Combine 8 cups of water and white vinegar in a large skillet; bring to a simmer. Break each egg into a custard cup, pour each gently into a pan. Cook 3 minutes or until desired degree of doneness. Remove eggs from pan, using a slotted spoon.

Place about ⅔ cup asparagus mixture on each of 4 plates. Sprinkle each serving with 1½ t of almonds; top each serving with 1 egg. Sprinkle evenly with Manchego cheese.

Serves four

Noodle Salad with Chicken & Chile-Scallion Oil

CHICKEN SCALLION OIL:
- 2 scallions, thinly sliced
- 2 garlic cloves, thinly sliced
- 2 star anise pods
- 2 T crushed fresh ginger
- 1 t Szechuan peppercorns
- ½ cup vegetable oil

NOODLES AND ASSEMBLY:
- 6 oz. wheat noodles
- 2 T reduced sodium soy sauce
- 2 T unseasoned rice vinegar
- 1 t sugar
- 1 t toasted sesame oil
- 2 cups shredded, cooked chicken
- 2 scallions, thinly sliced
- ½ cucumber, halved lengthwise, thinly sliced
- 4 radishes, trimmed, thinly sliced
- 1 cup cilantro leaves (or any sprout)

CHICKEN-SCALLION OIL – Cook all ingredients in a small saucepan over medium heat, swirling pan occasionally until scallions and garlic are just brown (about 3 minutes). Let cool; transfer oil to a jar. (Chile oil can be made 4 days ahead)

NOODLES AND ASSEMBLY – Cook noodles in a large pot of boiling water according to package directions; drain. Rinse noodles under cold water, then shake off as much water as possible. Whisk soy sauce, vinegar, sugar and oil in a medium bowl until sugar dissolves. Add noodles, chicken and scallions; toss to coat.

Toss with cucumber, radishes and cilantro and drizzle with chile oil just before serving.

DO AHEAD: Chile oil may be made 4 days in advance. Cover and chill.

Crunchy Kale, Apple & Pomegranate Salad

3 T shelled, unsalted pumpkin seeds
3 T red wine vinegar
¼ cup fat-free yogurt
6 cups Tuscan kale, washed & chopped into 1 in. pieces.
1 cup Granny Smith apples, diced into bite-size
½ cup pomegranate seeds
salt and crushed red pepper flakes

Place pumpkin seeds on a microwave safe plate and cook on high until they're a golden brown (about 2 minutes). Reserve.

Place vinegar and yogurt in a large mixing bowl and stir together. Put kale, apple, and pomegranate seeds in a bowl, toss together and add pumpkin seeds. Season with salt and crushed red pepper flakes.

Serves four

Seven Layer Caesar Salad

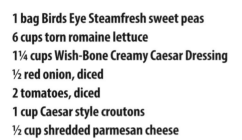

1 bag Birds Eye Steamfresh sweet peas
6 cups torn romaine lettuce
1¼ cups Wish-Bone Creamy Caesar Dressing
½ red onion, diced
2 tomatoes, diced
1 cup Caesar style croutons
½ cup shredded parmesan cheese

Cook Birds Eye Sweet Peas according to directions on pkg., and cool.

Layer lettuce, peas, Creamy Caesar Dressing, red onion, tomatoes, croutons and cheese in a large glass salad or truffle bowl.

Tasty Jell-O Salad

1 pkg. lime or lemon JELL-O (small)
⅔ cup boiling water
1 cup sugar
1 cup crushed pineapple, drained
1 cup cottage cheese
½ cup walnuts, chopped
1 cup whipped cream

Dissolve JELL-O in boiling water. Add sugar, stir and let stand until this congeals. Then, add pineapple, cottage cheese, walnuts and whipped cream. Mix well.

Pour into a ring mold or a pretty mold and refrigerate until set.

Chicken Salad with Haricots Verts

1 T fennel seeds
1 T Herbes de Provence
1 T kosher salt (plus more)
1 - 3½ to 4 pound chicken, patted dry
1 lb. small waxy potatoes (about 12)
8 oz. haricots verts, finely chopped
1 medium shallot, very finely chopped
½ garlic clove finely grated

2 T sherry or red wine vinegar
1 T Dijon mustard
¾ t chopped, fresh thyme
½ t sugar
⅓ cup olive oil
Freshly ground black pepper
2 radishes, thinly sliced
6 cups torn mixed tender salad greens

Coarsely grind fennel seeds, Herbes de Provence, and 1 T salt in spice mill. Rub chicken inside and out with spice mixture. Let sit at room temperature at least 1 hour.

Preheat oven to 425 degrees. Roast chicken in a roasting pan until an inserted thermometer in the thickest part of the thigh reads 165 degrees for 45-60 minutes. Let chicken rest at least 10 minutes before carving. When cool enough to handle, pull meat (including skin) into pieces.

While chicken is cooking, cook potatoes in water in a saucepan seasoned with salt. Cook until potatoes are tender (15-18 minutes). Let cool slightly then cut in half.

Return water to a boil and cook haricots verts until just tender (15-18 minutes). Transfer potatoes to a large bowl, let cool slightly. Then cut in half. Return water in the saucepan to a boil and cook haricot verts until just tender (about 5 minutes). Drain; transfer to bowl with potatoes. Meanwhile whisk shallot, garlic, vinegar, mustard, thyme, and sugar in a small bowl. Gradually whisk in oil, then 1 T water, season vinaigrette with salt and pepper. Add radishes, salad greens, and chicken to potatoes and haricot verts. Season with salt and pepper, drizzle with vinaigrette and toss to combine.

Skillet Asparagus Salad with Goat Cheese

1 t olive oil
¼ t freshly ground black pepper
⅛ t salt
1½ lbs. asparagus spears
1 cup water
2 t julienne cut orange rind
1 t julienne cut lemon rind

¼ cup fresh orange juice
1 t sugar
1 T dry white wine
1 ½ t fresh lemon juice
½ t Dijon mustard
¼ t freshly ground black pepper
⅛ t salt

5 t olive oil
2 cups mixed baby salad greens
½ cup goat cheese, crumbled
3 T chopped pecans, coated
1 T fresh tarragon leaves
1 t finely chopped fresh parsley
(flat leaf)

Combine first four ingredients in a large bowl; toss to coat. Heat a large cast iron skillet over medium-high heat. Add ⅓ of asparagus mixture; cook 4 minutes or until lightly charred and crisp tender, stirring occasionally. Remove from pan; set aside. Repeat procedure twice with remaining asparagus mixture. Place 1 cup water in a microwave safe measuring cup. Microwave at HIGH 2 minutes or until water just boils; add orange rind; let stand 20 seconds.

Drain, reserve rind; repeat procedure with lemon rind.
Combine orange rind, orange juice and sugar in a small sauce pan. Bring to a boil. Reduce heat to medium-low; cook until juice measures about 3 T. Combine wine, lemon juice, mustard, ¼ t pepper, and ⅛ t salt in a medium bowl; stir with a whisk. Gradually add 5 t oil, stirring constantly with a whisk. Stir in orange juice mixture.

Place ½ cup of greens on each of 6 plates. Divide asparagus evenly among salads. Top evenly with cheese, pecans and tarragon. Stir lemon rind, and parsley into orange juice mixture; drizzle dressing over salads. Serves six.

Red Rice Salad with Pecans, Fennel & Herbs

1 cup red rice
1 small fennel bulb, very thinly sliced
¼ medium red onion, thinly sliced
3 T fresh lime juice, divided
⅔ cup pecans, divided

¼ cup olive oil
½ cup cilantro leaves and finely chopped stems
Kosher salt and freshly ground black pepper
Toasted pistachio oil or almond oil

Cook rice according to pkg. directions. Spread out on a rimmed baking sheet; let cool. Meanwhile, toss fennel and onion with 2 T lime juice in a large bowl and let sit, tossing occasionally, until lime juice is almost entirely absorbed (10-15 minutes).

Coarsely chop 1/3 cup pecans; finely chop remaining nuts. Cook in olive oil in a small sauce pan over medium-low until golden brown (5-10 minutes). Let cool.

Add rice and pecans to fennel mixture along with remaining 1 T lime juice and toss to combine. Gently fold in cilantro; season with salt and pepper. Serve drizzled with pistachio oil if desired.

DO AHEAD: Rice salad without pistachio can be chilled up to 1 day. Bring to room temperature before serving.

Roasted Citrus & Avocado Salad

1 blood or Valencia orange, sliced ⅛ in. thick, seeds removed
1 lemon, seeds removed, sliced ⅛ in. thick
4 T olive oil, divided
Kosher salt and freshly ground pepper
¼ small red onion thinly sliced
2 T fresh lemon juice
1 bunch arugula or watercress, thick stems trimmed
½ cup fresh mint leaves
1 avocado, cut into wedges

Preheat oven to 425 degrees. Toss lemon and orange slices with 1 T oil on rimmed baking sheet; season with salt and pepper. Roast citrus, tossing occasionally, until lightly charred in spots (10-15 minutes). Let cool.

Meanwhile, combine onion and lemon juice in a large bowl; season with salt and pepper and let sit 5 minutes. Add roasted citrus to bowl with onion along with arugula and mint.

Drizzle remaining 3 T of oil, over; toss with salt and pepper again and toss everything to combine and coat. Add avocado and very gently toss until lightly dressed. (You don't want to crush the avocado.)

Chicken, Kale, Apple & Pancetta Salad

1½ t Dijon mustard
1½ t red wine vinegar
½ t fresh-squeezed lemon juice
¼ cup extra-virgin olive oil
salt and pepper
1½ cups baby kale
½ cup spinach
⅓ cup shaved Parmigiano-Reggiano
1 red radish, thinly sliced
⅓ cup of sliced apple
4 oz. grilled chicken breast, sliced
1 T diced pancetta, pan-fried and drained

In a small bowl, whisk together the Dijon mustard, red wine vinegar, lemon juice and extra-virgin olive oil. Season to taste with salt and pepper.

Put the kale and spinach in a bowl. Toss with 1½–2 t. olive oil, radish, apple, and half the cheese. Top with slices of chicken, pancetta, and the remaining cheese.

Mu Shu Chicken Salad

2 t canola oil
1 bag (10 oz.) coleslaw mix
¾ cup shredded carrot
¾ cup mu shu stir fry sauce
4 cups shredded rotisserie chicken
8 cups Asian salad blend
3 scallions, sliced
⅓ cup unsalted peanuts

Heat oil in a non-stick skillet over medium-high heat. Add coleslaw mix and carrot; cook for 5 minutes, stirring occasionally until partially wilted. Stir in ½ cup of the sauce and bring to a simmer; stir in chicken.

To serve, place greens on a large, serving platter. Spoon chicken mixture over greens and sprinkle with scallions and peanuts. Serve remaining ¼ cup stir-fry sauce on the side for drizzling over salad.

Steak Salad with Caraway Vinaigrette & Rye Croutons

2 slices seeded rye bread, torn into
  ¼" pieces
3 T plus ¼ cup olive oil, divided
1½ lbs. hanger steak, cut into 4 pieces*
Kosher salt and freshly ground black pepper
1 t caraway seeds
1 T sherry vinegar

1 T whole grain mustard
½ t honey
4 small carrots, peeled, shaved lengthwise
4 cups mustard greens, ribs removed,
  bite-sized pieces
1 cup parsley leaves with tender stems
*Center membranes removed

Preheat oven to 400 degrees. Toss bread with 2 T oil a rimmed baking sheet and toast, tossing halfway through, until golden brown, 8-10 minutes, set aside.

Meanwhile, heat 1 T oil in a large skillet over medium heat high heat. Season steak with salt and pepper and cook, turning occasionally, 8-10 minutes for medium-rare. Transfer to a cutting board; let rest 5 minutes before slicing.

Toast caraway seeds in a small dry skillet over medium heat, tossing until fragrant (about 2 minutes). Let cool.

Whisk caraway, vinegar, mustard and honey and remaining ¼ cup of oil in a large bowl; season with salt and pepper. Add carrots, mustard greens, parsley and steak and toss. Serve salad topped with reserved croutons.

Strawberry-Rhubarb Salad with Mint & Hazelnuts

½ **cup blanched hazelnuts**
2 rhubarb stalks, thinly sliced on the diagonal
2 T sugar
2 T fresh orange juice
1 T fresh lemon juice
2 pounds fresh strawberries, hulled, quartered
¼ **cup fresh mint leaves, torn**

Preheat oven to 350 degrees. Toast hazelnuts on a rimmed baking sheet, tossing occasionally, until golden brown, 8-10 minutes. Let cool; then chop.

Meanwhile toss, rhubarb, sugar, orange juice and lemon juice in a medium bowl. Let sit until rhubarb is slightly softened and releases its juices; about 30 minutes. Toss with hazelnuts, mint, and strawberries.

Crunchy Kale & Quinoa Salad

1½ cups uncooked quinoa
½ cup toasted pecans, chopped
⅓ bunch of basil, chopped
⅓ bunch of flat leaf parsley, chopped
½ cup dried cherries (no sugar added)
2 celery stalks, chopped
2 carrots, chopped
4 cups chopped kale, stems removed
¼ cup crumbled feta cheese
¼ cup olive oil
¼ cup fresh lemon juice
Kosher salt to taste

Bring a large pot of salted water to a boil. Add the quinoa and return to a boil.
Cook until al dente, as you would pasta, 10-11 minutes. Drain well and cool.

Combine all the remaining ingredients in a large bowl and toss. Add the cooled quinoa and
toss.

Lobster Salad with Potatoes & Pickled Onion

1 12 oz. bottle pale lager
2 -1½ pound live lobsters
1 pound potatoes
1 T kosher salt plus more
¼ cup red wine vinegar
1 T sugar

½ medium red onion, thinly sliced
2 T fresh lemon juice
¼ cup olive oil, plus more for drizzling
½ cup fresh mint leaves
2 cups frieze (optional)
Freshly ground black pepper

Bring beer to a boil in a large heavy pot. Add lobsters, cover and steam until shells are bright red and meat is cooked thoroughly (10-12 minutes). Remove from pot with tongs and let cool 10 minutes. Crack shells, remove meat from tail, claws and knuckles.

Meanwhile, place potatoes in a large saucepan and add enough water to cover by 2 inches. Season with salt. Bring to a boil and cook until tender, 10-12 minutes; drain. Transfer potatoes to a large bowl and lightly crush with a fork. Bring vinegar, sugar, 1 T salt, and ½ cup water to a simmer in a small sauce pan. Add onion, remove from heat, and let sit 5 minutes; drain. Let pickled onion cool.

Whisk lemon juice and ½ cup of oil in a medium bowl; season with salt. Add mint, pickled onion, potatoes, and lobster meat; toss to combine. Add frieze and toss to combine. Drizzle with more oil; season with more lemon juice and pepper.

DO AHEAD: Lobsters may be cooked and meat removed 2 days ahead, cover meat and chill. Onions and potatoes may be cooked 1 day ahead; cover and chill. Bring potatoes to room temperature before using.

Salad with Candied Pecans, Pears & Blue Cheese

1 cup pecan halves
¼ cup brown sugar
1 T olive oil
1 T balsamic vinegar

DRESSING INGREDIENTS
2 t lemon juice
1 t balsamic vinegar
½ t Dijon mustard
3 T olive oil

salt and pepper to taste
8 cups mixed greens
3 oz. crumbled blue cheese
2 ripe pears, peeled and
    thinly sliced

CANDIED PECANS:

Prepare a large sheet of parchment paper or foil for cooling pecans.

Stir sugar, oil, and vinegar in a large skillet over medium heat until sugar melts and syrup bubbles, about 3 minutes. Mix in pecans and stir until nuts are toasted and syrup coats them evenly (5-6 minutes). Turn nuts out onto prepared parchment paper and separate using two forks. Cool completely.

DRESSING DIRECTIONS

In a small bowl, mix lemon juice, balsamic vinegar, and Dijon mustard with a fork until well blended. Pour in the olive oil in a slow, steady stream, whisking constantly. Whisk until well combined. Season with salt and pepper.

SALAD ASSEMBLY DIRECTION:

Put the greens into a big bowl and toss with the dressing and salt to taste. Only use as much dressing as you need to coat the greens lightly (otherwise, the acid in the dressing will wilt them). Arrange salad on plates, top with pears, pecans and cheese.

Shaved Melon Salad with Lemon-Sherry Dressing

1 t grated lemon rind
2 T fresh lemon juice
1 T sherry
1 t honey
⅜ t kosher salt
¼ t freshly ground black pepper
2 T extra virgin olive oil
½ medium cantaloupe
½ medium honeydew melon
3 T fresh mint

Combine first 6 ingredients in a large bowl, stirring with a whisk. Gradually add oil, stirring constantly with a whisk.

Remove and discard seeds from the cantaloupe and honeydew melon. Cut melons into 2 inch wide wedges; remove rinds. Cut melon wedges into long, thin ribbons. Add melon ribbons to dressing; toss gently to coat. Sprinkle with mint. Serve immediately.

Farro, Cherry & Walnut Salad

5 cups water
1½ cups uncooked farro
½ t salt, divided
¾ pound sweet cherries, pitted and halved
⅔ cup diced celery
½ cup coarsely chopped walnuts, toasted
¼ cup packed fresh flat-leaf parsley leaves
2 T fresh lemon juice
1 T whole-grain Dijon mustard
1 T honey
¼ t freshly ground black pepper
3 T extra-virgin olive oil

Bring 5 cups of water to a boil in a large saucepan. Add farro and ¼ t salt to boiling water; cook 15 minutes. Drain; cool at room temperature 15 minutes. Combine farro, cherries, walnuts, celery, and parsley in a large bowl.

Combine lemon juice, mustard, honey, pepper and remaining ¼ t salt, stirring constantly with a whisk. Gradually add oil, stirring constantly with a whisk. Pour dressing over farro mixture; toss to coat.

Cucumber & Herb Salad with Pine Nuts

1 T lemon rind strips
2 T fresh lemon juice
1 T extra virgin olive oil
½ t kosher salt
¼ t freshly ground black pepper
¼ cup coarsely chopped flat-leaf parsley leaves
¼ cup coarsely chopped celery leaves
4 green onions, thinly sliced
3 cups coarsely chopped or sliced cucumber
2 T pine nuts, toasted

Combine first 5 ingredients in a medium bowl, stirring with a whisk. Add parsley, celery leaves, onions, and cucumber; toss gently. Sprinkle with pine nuts.

Summer Veggie Salad Green Onion & Dill Quinoa

4 (4 in.) portabella mushroom caps
1 (1/2 in. thick) slices red onion
2 ears shucked corn
1 large red bell pepper, quartered & seeded
1 medium zucchini, halved lengthwise
1 large yellow squash, halved lengthwise
Cooking spray
2 T olive oil

2 t fresh lemon juice
1 t minced fresh thyme
½ t Dijon mustard
¼ t kosher salt
¼ t freshly ground black pepper
2 oz. Manchego cheese, shaved (½ cup)
1 oz. pine nuts toasted (about ¼ cup)

Preheat grill to medium high heat. Coat mushrooms, onion, corn, bell pepper, zucchini, and yellow squash with cooking spray. Arrange vegetable on grill rack coated with cooking spray. Grill 5 minutes on each side or until tender.

Combine oil and next 5 ingredients (through black pepper) in a large bowl, stirring with a whisk. Cut kernels from ears of corn, add to oil mixture. Cut remaining vegetables into bite-size pieces; add to oil mixture. Toss gently to combine. Top with cheese and pine nuts.

Grilled Lemon-Dijon Chicken Thighs with Arugula Salad

4 (4 oz.) skinless boneless chicken thighs
½ t salt, divided
¼ t freshly ground black pepper, divided
2 ½ T extra virgin olive oil, divided
2 t fresh lemon juice
2 t Dijon mustard
1 t minced fresh garlic

Cooking spray
2 T thinly sliced shallots
1 T balsamic vinegar
2 t honey
1 cup grape-size tomatoes
1 (5 oz. pkg.) baby arugula

Sprinkle chicken with ¼ T salt and ⅛ pepper. Combine chicken 1 ½ t oil, juice, Dijon, and garlic in a bowl; toss to coat. Let stand 4 minutes. Heat a grill pan over medium-high heat. Coat pan with cooking spray. Add chicken to pan, grill 5 minutes on each side or until done. Place chicken on a cutting board. Cut chicken into ¼ inch thick slices.

Combine remaining ¼ t salt, remaining ⅛ t pepper, remaining 2 T oil, shallots, vinegar, and honey in a large bowl, stirring with a whisk to dissolve honey. Add tomatoes and arugula mixture to each of 4 plates; top evenly with sliced chicken.

Serves four

Pea-In-A-Pod Princess Salad

2 cups shelled fresh green peas
½ cup extra virgin olive oil
3 T balsamic or sherry vinegar
¼ t salt
Freshly ground pepper
3 slices bacon
2 slices crispy bread, cubed
2 cups fresh torn lettuce leaves
2 oz. grated Parmigiano cheese

Boil peas 6 minutes. Drain and rinse with cold water. Combine olive oil, balsamic vinegar, salt and pepper, whisk well. Cook bacon until crispy. Remove from pan. Toss bread cubes in drippings and cook until crispy. Combine peas, lettuce, vinaigrette, and croutons. Top with cheese.

Serves four

Farro Salad with Roasted Beets, Watercress & Poppyseed Dressing

2 bunches small beets, trimmed
⅓ cup uncooked farro
3 cups of water
¾ kosher salt, divided
3 cups trimmed watercress
½ cup thinly sliced red onion
2 oz. crumbled goat cheese (about ½ cup)
2 T cider vinegar
2 T toasted walnut oil
2 T reduced fat poppyseed dressing

Combine all ingredients in a large bowl with a whisk.

Apple & Walnut Salad

DRESSING INGREDIENTS
¼ cup extra virgin olive oil
3 T fresh lemon juice
2 T cider vinegar
1 T spicy brown mustard

MIX-INS
1 green apple, cored and very thinly sliced
⅔ cup, walnuts, chopped
½ cup sharp cheese, shredded

In small jar or container with lid; combine the dressing ingredients. Close lid tightly and shake until well combined.

Toss one 5 oz. bag mixed salad greens with mix-ins.

Drizzle salad with dressing and toss to combine.

Arugula Salad with Honey-Clementine Vinaigrette

SALAD INGREDIENTS:

4–½ cups arugula, kale, or spinach or
   combinations
½ cup pomegranate seeds
½ cup dried cranberries
3 clementines or 2 naval oranges peeled
   and segmented
4 T lightly salted pistachios chopped
   (shells removed)
3 T sunflower or pepitas seeds
⅓ cup parmigiano shavings or crumbled
   goat cheese

HONEY-CLEMENTINE VINAIGRETTE
INGREDIENTS:

Juice of 3 clementines or substitute with
fresh orange juice
6 T extra-virgin olive oil
2 T honey
3 t white balsamic vinegar or
   pomegranate Quince
1 garlic clove, minced
Salt and pepper to taste

Divide the arugula evenly among bowls. Place the sunflower seeds in a small dry skillet and toast over medium heat until golden brown. Meanwhile, sprinkle the chopped pistachio and pomegranate seeds over the arugula. When the sunflower seeds are nice and toasty, add them to the salads. Add in clementine segments, cranberries, and top each salad with Parmesan shavings.

TO MAKE THE VINAIGRETTE:
Whisk all the ingredients together in a bowl, use a Mason jar and shake to combine. Store leftovers in a refrigerator.

Citrus Salad with Tarragon

¼ cup sugar
¼ cup fresh tarragon leaves (packed)*
4 blood oranges
4 clementines
2 naval oranges
2 tangerines
*Plus more for serving

Combine sugar, ¼ cup tarragon, and ¼ cup of water in a jar, cover and shake until sugar is dissolved. Strain tarragon syrup through a fine mesh sieve into a clean jar or small bowl; discard tarragon.

Use a sharp knife, remove peel and oranges, clementines, and tangerines; discard. Slice citrus crosswise into ¼ inch thick rounds. Arrange citrus on a platter, drizzle with tarragon syrup (if your citrus is sweet, you may not want to use all of the syrup), and top with more tarragon leaves.

Serves eight

Green Mango Salad

2 Thai green or red chilies with seeds removed
1 garlic clove, chopped
½ cup (or more) fresh lime juice
¼ cup fish sauce
2 T vegetable oil
2 t palm or brown sugar
4 green mangoes
2 medium shallots, thinly sliced
½ cup unsalted dry roasted, coarsely chopped
½ cup fresh cilantro leaves
¼ cup fresh mint leaves
2 toasted, dried shrimp (optional)
2 T toasted sesame seeds
Kosher salt

Purée chilies, garlic, lime juice, fish sauce, vegetable oil, and palm or brown sugar in a blender until smooth. Toss mangos, shallots, peanuts, cilantro, mint, dried shrimp, sesame seeds, and dressing in a large bowl; season salad with salt.

Waldorf Salad with Lemon Vinaigrette

¼ cup fresh lemon juice
2 T agave syrup
1 cup grapeseed oil
Kosher salt
Freshly ground black pepper
1 Red Delicious apple, cut into ⅛ inch slices
1 Granny Smith apple, cut into ⅛ inch slices
¼ cup red and green seedless grapes, halved
2 ribs celery with leaves, chopped
1 head romaine lettuce
½ cup candied walnuts
walnut oil

Pour lemon juice and agave syrup into a blender; combine until mixture has a froth to it. Slowly pour in the grape seed oil until it begins to thicken. Add salt and pepper to taste.

Place apples, grapes and celery in a large bowl and toss with enough lemon vinaigrette to cover. Let sit and taste for seasoning. Add lettuce and toss well.

Distribute salad mixture among 4 to 6 plates and sprinkle walnuts on top.
Drizzle with walnut oil.

Herring Salad
(Swedish Translation: Sillsallad)

1 large salt-water herring
1 cup cooked or pickled beets, diced
1¼ cup cooked potatoes, diced
1 cup diced roast beef or ham
1 medium sweet pickle, finely chopped
1 apple, medium, peeled, cored and diced

2 T vinegar
1 t vinegar
⅛ t white pepper
1 hard-boiled egg; cut white into strips,
  mash yolk
¼ cup whipping cream (whipped)

Soak the herring in water overnight. Remove skin and bones. Chop fairly fine. Mix herring, diced beets, diced potatoes, meat, diced apple, chopped pickle, and add vinegar, sugar and pepper.

Turn out on a platter and garnish with mashed egg yolk in center with egg white strips arranged in a spiral around the yolk. You may also add parsley and small cooked beets for decoration. Serve with either whipped or sour cream. Some prefer to stir ice cream into the salad before it is placed on the platter.

Serves four to six

Citrus Ambrosia Salad

2 each of the following; naval oranges & red grapefruit*
4 clementines, peeled, cut crosswise into thin slices
1 cup miniature marshmallows
½ cup Baker's Angel Flake Coconut, toasted
½ cup pomegranate seeds
½ cup Brakestone's reduced fat or Knutsen sour cream
1 T honey
Peeled, cut crosswise into thin slices

Cut orange and grapefruit slices into quarters; arrange alternately on large plate with clementine slices. Top with marshmallows, coconut, and pomegranate seeds. Mix remaining ingredients; drizzle over fruit just before serving.

HOW TO TOAST COCONUT:
Spread Baker's Angel Flake Coconut evenly in a shallow baking pan. Bake at 350 degrees for 7 to 10 minutes, or until light brown, stirring frequently.

Sukiyaki Mushroom Salad

2 T butter
½ pound sliced, fresh mushrooms
½ green pepper, thinly sliced
½ small onion, thinly sliced
2 t reduced sukiyaki sauce
2 t reduced sodium soy sauce
4 lettuce leaves
2 bacon strips, cooked and crumbled

In a non-stick skillet, melt butter. Add the mushrooms, green pepper, onion, sukiyaki sauce and soy sauce; sauté for 5 minutes or until vegetables are crisp-tender. Spoon onto lettuce leaves. Sprinkle with bacon.

Serves two

Grilled Bread Salad with Sweet Peppers & Onions

¼ loaf country style bread, crust removed*
6 T olive oil, divided
Kosher salt, freshly ground pepper
2 large red bell peppers, halved,
    ribs & seeds removed
2 small red onions; peeled, quartered,
    some root

3 T red wine or sherry vinegar
½ t paprika, preferably smoked
2 T coarsely chopped chives, plus more
    for serving
*Bread torn in large pieces

Prepare grill for medium high heat. Toss bread with 2 T oil in a medium bowl. Season with salt and pepper. Toss bell peppers and onions with 2 T oil; Season with salt and pepper. Grill bread, turning occasionally, until golden brown (8-10 minutes). Transfer to plate. Grill vegetables, turning often, until very tender and charred in spots. Transfer to a cutting board.

Trim root end from onions and separate layers. Transfer to a bowl, add vinegar and paprika; toss to coat. Remove as much skin as possible from peppers, discard. Cut into ¼ inch strips. Add peppers, grilled bread, 2 T chives, & remaining 2 T oil to bowl with onions and toss. Season with salt and pepper. Serve topped with more chives.

Serves four

Summer Squash Salad

2 cups torn lettuce
⅓ cup thinly sliced zucchini
⅓ cup thinly sliced summer squash
3 radishes, sliced
¼ cup Italian salad dressing

In a bowl, toss the lettuce, zucchini, yellow squash and radishes. Serve with dressing.

Serves two

Spiral Pasta Salad

1 cup cooked spiral pasta
⅓ cup halved grape size tomatoes
¼ cup quartered sliced cucumber
¼ cup quartered sliced sweet onion
¼ cup sliced, ripe olives
3 T grated Parmesan cheese
¼ cup Ranch salad dressing

In a bowl, combine the first six ingredients. Add dressing and toss to coat.

Cover and refrigerate until serving.

Serves two

Zippy Radish Salad

1 cup thinly sliced radishes
¼ cup cubed Swiss cheese
1 green onion, sliced
1½ tarragon vinegar
¼ t minced garlic
¼ t Dijon mustard
⅛ t salt; dash of pepper
4 t olive oil

In a bowl, combine the radishes, cheese and onion. In a small bowl, combine the vinegar, garlic, mustard, salt and pepper; whisk in oil with smooth. Pour over radish mixture and toss to coat. Chill until serving. Serve on a bed of lettuce.

Serves two

Caramelized Squash Salad with Pistachios & Goat Cheese

1 cup orange juice
3 T pure maple syrup
1½ T Dijon mustard
1 T grated fresh ginger
1½ lbs. butternut squash*
½ t salt

¼ t ground black pepper
⅓ cup olive oil
6 cups mixed salad greens
1 small head of radicchio,
    cored & sliced

½ cup roasted & salted
    pistachio nuts
3 oz. goat cheese, crumbled
Peeled, halved crosswise, seeded
and cut into ½ inch strips

For a marinade; in a small bowl, stir together orange juice, maple syrup, mustard and ginger. Set aside ½ cup of marinade. Place butternut pieces in a large resealable plastic bag set in a shallow dish. Pour remaining marinade over squash. Seal bag; turn to coat squash. Marinate in refrigerator for 1 to 4 hours, turning occasionally.

Preheat oven to 400 degrees. Coat a large baking sheet with cooking spray; set aside. Drain and discard marinade from squash. Place squash on prepared baking sheet. Roast squash 25–30 minutes or until tender (lightly brown in spots). Set aside.

For dressing, whisk together the reserved salt, marinade, and pepper. Slowly whisk in the oil. Drizzle 2 to 3 T of the dressing over warm squash; Toss to combine.
In a bowl, combine the mixed greens, radicchio, and ½ the nuts.
Toss with half the dressing. Toss roasted squash into salad.
Top with remaining nuts and goat cheese and remaining dressing.

Serves six

Pineapple Turkey Salad

2 T canola oil, divided
1 t minced fresh ginger root
1 garlic clove, minced
1 turkey breast tenderloin; ½ inch slices
1 cup fresh cauliflowerets

½ medium sweet red pepper, chopped
3 green onions, sliced
1 fresh pineapple
2 cups chopped fresh spinach
2 T apricot nectar

In a non-stick skillet, heat 1 t oil, ginger, and garlic. Add turkey, stir-fry 8 to 10 minutes or until no longer pink. Remove turkey and keep warm. Add remaining oil to the skillet; stir-fry 1 minute longer.

Cut pineapple in half and remove fruit, leaving 1-inch shells; set shells aside for serving. Cut fruit into cubes; set aside 1½ cups (refrigerate remaining pineapple for another use). In a large bowl, combine the turkey, vegetables, spinach and reserved pineapple. In a small bowl, whisk the apricot nectar, vinegar, and pepper; add to turkey salad and toss to coat. Serve in pineapple shells.

Serves two

Notes

CHAPTER 2

Dressings

Fruit Salad Dressing

1½ t. all purpose flour
1 can (6 oz.) pineapple juice
⅓ cup sugar
⅓ cup orange juice concentrate
2 T honey
2 T lemon juice
Assorted fresh fruit

In a saucepan, combine the first six ingredients. Bring to a boil; cook and stir for 2 minutes or until thickened and bubbly. Cool. Serve over fruit.

Leftover dressing may be refrigerated up to one week.

Classic Vinaigrette Dressing

½ cup olive oil
3–4 T fresh lemon juice
1 t Dijon mustard
¼ t salt
¼ t freshly ground black pepper

Whisk all ingredients together. Toss with greens or potato salad.

After making vinaigrette dressing, add ⅓ cup crumbled blue cheese, 3 slices bacon, crumbled, and 2 T chopped celery.

Creamy Poppyseed Dressing

Contributed by Linsey Friesz

½ cup mayonnaise
¼ cup sour cream
2½ T white wine vinegar
2 T poppyseeds
3 T sugar

Whisk ingredients together and add milk until desired thickness is achieved.

Bistro Bacon Salad Dressing Recipe

DIRECTIONS FOR MAKING VINAIGRETTE DRESSING

½ cup olive oil
3–4 T fresh lemon juice
1 t Dijon mustard
¼ t salt
¼ t freshly ground black pepper

Make classic vinaigrette dressing (as above).

Whisk all ingredients together and toss with greens or potato salad. After making vinaigrette dressing, add ⅓ cup crumbled blue cheese, 3 slices bacon, crumbled, and 2 T chopped celery.

Mediterranean Salad Dressing

DIRECTIONS FOR MAKING VINAIGRETTE DRESSING

½ cup olive oil
3-4 T fresh lemon juice
1 t Dijon mustard
¼ t salt
¼ t freshly ground pepper

Prepare vinaigrette dressing. Whisk all ingredients together. Toss with greens or potato salad. Mash in ½ cup crumbled feta. Then whisk in 1 T chopped parsley, 1 t oregano, and 1 T diced plum tomato.

Dijon Salad Dressing

3 T Dijon mustard
3 T champagne vinegar
½ t each salt and pepper (to taste)
½ cup olive oil

Whisk 3 T each Dijon mustard and champagne vinegar, ½ t each of salt and pepper (to taste). Gradually whisk in ½ cup olive oil.

Spicy Honey Mustard Salad Dressing

2 T lime juice
2 T honey
2 T Dijon mustard
½ t each lime zest and kosher salt
¼ cup olive oil
¼ cup vegetable oil
2 t chopped thyme

Gradually whisk in ¼ cup each of olive oil and vegetable oil. Then add 2 t chopped thyme and ½ t minced jalapeño.

Mango Lime Salad Dressing

1 chopped, seeded mango
Zest and juice of 1 lime
1 t each Dijon mustard and sugar*
¼ cup rice vinegar
½ cup vegetable oil
1 t kosher salt*
*Blend Dijon mustard, sugar, and kosher salt in a blender

In a blender, process the juice and zest of a lime, a chopped and peeled mango and 1 t each of Dijon mustard, ¼ cup of rice vinegar, and ½ cup vegetable oil.

Italian Soak Salad Dressing

2 T minced red onion (15 minutes in cold water)
½ garlic clove
2 T fresh parsley
1 t dried oregano
½ t kosher salt
2 T red wine vinegar

Drain minced onion. Place first 4 ingredients on a board. Chop and mash into a paste. Whisk with 2 T red wine vinegar and the onion. Gradually whisk in ½ cup olive oil.

Lemon-Dill Salad Dressing

2 T lemon juice
2 T chopped dill
2 T Dijon mustard
1 t lemon zest

½ t sugar (or to taste)
Salt to taste
¼ cup each olive oil and vegetable oil

Whisk together all ingredients.

Green Goddess Salad Dressing

1 t lemon zest
¼ cup lemon juice
1 T finely chopped fresh dill
¾ t kosher salt

½ t Dijon mustard
¼ t sugar
Finely ground black pepper
6 T canola oil

Place all ingredients in a medium bowl and whisk to combine. Taste and season with pepper as needed.

Boiled Salad Dressing

1 cup vinegar
¾ cup sugar
1 rounded T flour
1 t dry mustard
1 egg
Pinch of salt

Heat vinegar, and then add other ingredients. Boil until thick.

Celery Seed Salad Dressing

½ cup sugar
1 t dry mustard
1 t salt
¼ small onion, grated
⅓ cup vinegar
1 T celery seeds
1 cup salad oil

Mix all but the oil and beat. Then add the oil SLOWLY, a little at a time.

Martha Stewart's Favorite Salad Dressing Recipe

¾ cup extra virgin olive oil
¼ cup white wine vinegar
1 T Dijon mustard
½ t walnut oil
¼ salt
⅛ t pepper

Combine all ingredients.

Olive Garden Salad Dressing

½ cup mayonnaise
⅓ cup white vinegar
1 t vegetable oil
2 T corn syrup
2 T Parmesan cheese

2 T Roman cheese
¼ t garlic salt
½ t parsley flakes
1 T lemon juice

Mix all ingredients in a blender until well mixed. Add sugar to meet personal taste.

Spinach-Cabbage Salad Dressing

1 cup spinach, chopped
1 cup cabbage, chopped
½ cup white vinegar
½ cup mayonnaise

Toss, to coat well, all ingredients.

Onion French Salad Dressing

1 can tomato soup (10 oz.)
1 cup vegetable oil
¾ cup apple cider vinegar
1 small onion, grated
¼ cup sugar
1 clove garlic, minced
1 T Dijon mustard
1 T horseradish
1 t salt
1 t black pepper

Combine all ingredients.

Greek Salad Dressing

2 fresh garlic cloves, minced and crushed
¼ t salt
1½ t Dijon mustard
½ cup extra virgin olive oil
2 T fresh lemon juice
½ t sugar
5 T red wine vinegar
½ t basil leaves (optional)

Mix all ingredients together and shake well to mix.

Cucumber Yogurt Dressing

1 cup chopped seeded peeled cucumber
3 T plain low fat yogurt
2 T olive oil
1 T balsamic vinegar
¼ t salt
¼ t black pepper
⅛ T diced dill

Combine all ingredients.

Creamy Italian Dressing

¼ cup mayonnaise
1 T milk
1 T cider vinegar
½ t oregano
½ t basil
½ t rosemary
¼ t sugar
½ t garlic powder
⅛ t pepper

In a jar with a tight fitting lid, combine all ingredients. Shake well.

Benihana Ginger Salad Dressing

½ cup onion, minced
½ cup peanut oil
⅓ cup rice vinegar
2 T water
2 T fresh ginger, minced
2 T celery, minced
2 T ketchup
4 t soy sauce
2 t lemon juice
½ t garlic, minced
½ t salt
¼ t pepper

Combine all ingredients in a blender. Blend on high speed for about 30 seconds or until the ginger is well puréed.

Spinach Salad with Warm Bacon Dressing

8 oz. young spinach
2 large eggs
8 pieces thick-sliced bacon
3 T red wine vinegar
1 t sugar
½ t Dijon mustard
Kosher salt
Finely ground black pepper
4 large white mushrooms, sliced
1 small onion, sliced thin

Remove stems from spinach, wash and drain. Boil eggs. Once water comes to a boil, turn off heat and leave eggs in water 15 minutes. Remove from heat and peel off shell. Slice each egg into 8 pieces.
Fry bacon and remove to a paper towel to cool.

Transfer fat to a small saucepan over low heat and whisk in red wine vinegar, sugar and Dijon mustard. Small pinch each of salt and pepper.

Add mushrooms and sliced bacon to the spinach and toss. Add bacon and dressing and toss. Divide spinach between 4 plates and divide eggs among them.

Awesome Red Wine Vinaigrette Salad Dressing

½ cup canola or vegetable oil
¼ cup red wine vinegar
¼ cup sugar
¼ t salt
¼ t paprika
1 t white pepper
1 garlic clove, pressed

Add all ingredients in a jar with a tight lid. Shake vigorously.

Store in a refrigerator up to 1 week. Shake to recombine before using.

Blueberry-Vinaigrette Salad Dressing

1 cup fresh or frozen blueberries
¼ cup vegetable oil
2 t orange marmalade
2 t lemon juice
1 t Dijon mustard
¼ t salt

In a blender container, combine ½ of the blueberries with the other ingredients. Blend until a smooth, thick dressing forms.

Drizzle dressing over salad and sprinkle with remaining blueberries.

Lemon Balsamic Salad Dressing

2 T balsamic vinegar
1 T lemon juice
2 t Dijon mustard
½ kosher salt
Pepper to taste
½ cup olive oil

Whisk together first 5 ingredients to taste. Gradually whisk in olive oil

Four-Herb Green Goddess Dressing

1 cup plain fat-free Greek yogurt
½ cup fat free mayonnaise
2 t Worcestershire sauce
2 t fresh lemon juice
½ t Tabasco

3 canned anchovy fillets
1 garlic clove, minced
⅔ cup fresh parsley leaves
¼ cup fresh tarragon leaves
¼ cup fresh chives

Place first 7 ingredients in a blender or food processor; process until smooth. Add parsley and remaining ingredients; process until herbs are minced.

Hail Caesar Salad Dressing

1 loaf old Italian bread
3 garlic cloves, minced
9 T extra virgin olive oil
¼ t plus one pinch kosher salt
2 eggs
2 heads romaine lettuce (small leaves only)
7 grinds black pepper
1 lemon, juiced
8 drops Worcestershire sauce
¼ cup grated parmesan cheese

Cut ½ to ¾ inch croutons from the loaf of bread. Use a mortar and pestle to mash garlic with olive oil.

Bring 2 cups of water to a boil in a small saucepan. Add eggs and let cook 1 minute.

In a bowl, tear lettuce and toss with 3 T olive oil. Toss and sprinkle with remaining salt and pepper. Add remaining olive oil and toss well. Toss with remaining ingredients.

Creamy Cracked Pink Pepper Salad Dressing

1 peeled cucumber
2 T fresh lemon juice
1 T nutritional yeast
1 t pink cracked peppercorns
2 dates
Salt to taste

Place everything but the peppercorns in the blender and mix at high speed.

Pour the dressing into a usable container and add the peppercorns.

Strawberry-Vinaigrette Salad Dressing

1 cup sugar-free strawberry preserves
¼ cup balsamic vinegar
¼ cup Dijon mustard
½ t ground red pepper
½ cup olive oil
½ cup water

In a medium bowl, whisk together the preserves, vinegar, mustard and pepper until thoroughly combined.

Gradually whisk in olive oil and then water. Serve immediately or keep chilled until served.

Creamy Dill Salad Dressing

1 12.3 oz. pkg. silken tofu
2 T lemon juice
3 T seasoned rice vinegar
1 T cider vinegar
1 t garlic ground or in powder
½ t dried dill weed
¼ t salt

Combine all ingredients (may use blender). Blend until completely smooth (1 to 2 minutes). Store any extra dressing in an air-tight container in the refrigerator.

Balsamic Vinaigrette Salad Dressing

4 T balsamic vinegar
4 T season rice vinegar
2 T ketchup
2 t stone-ground mustard
2 garlic cloves, pressed

Whisk first four ingredients together. Add garlic cloves.

Kraft's Catalina Salad Dressing

INGREDIENTS FOR 2 CUPS

1 cup sugar
2 t salt
1 dash paprika
½ t chili powder
½ t celery seed
½ t dry mustard
Grated onion to taste
½ cup vinegar
⅔ cup ketchup
1 cup vegetable oil

Place all ingredients into a blender and mix. Store in a jar in the refrigerator. Shake before using.

Chunky Blue Cheese Salad Dressing

1 cup mayonnaise
1 cup sour cream
½ cup buttermilk
½ t white pepper
2 T grated onions
4 dashes Tabasco sauce
1 T lemon juice
1 dash cayenne pepper
1 t minced garlic
1 t sugar
6 oz. crumbled blue cheese

Combine mayonnaise, sour cream, and buttermilk, mixing well.

Add remaining ingredients, mixing well.

Must refrigerate 24 hours before serving for best flavor.

Garlic Spinach Salad Dressing

1 T olive oil
1 clove fresh garlic
1 cup organic baby spinach

Use a skillet or deep stock pot. Add spinach, use more than you think as it really shrinks. Add olive oil. Add minced garlic, let it cook for 1 minute. Let spinach wilt down but don't let it get dark. The brighter the better – lots of vitamins!

Mediterranean Mint Tea Salad Dressing

1 cup extra-virgin olive oil
½–¾ cup sugar (personal taste)
⅓ cup gluten-free ketchup
¼ cup apple cider vinegar
1 t Worcestershire sauce

Combine all ingredients in a bowl and whisk until sugar is dissolved and dressing is smooth and glossy. Store in a container with a tight-fitting lid and refrigerate.

Oriental Salad Dressing

¼ **cup soy sauce**
¼ **cup rice vinegar**
¼ **cup water**
¼ **t minced fresh garlic**
¼ **t minced fresh ginger**

Combine all ingredients in a covered jar. Shake to mix. Store in a covered jar in the refrigerator.

To make into a Dijon mustard dressing, add 2 t Dijon mustard.

Mcdougall's Vinaigrette Salad Dressing

For ¾ cup of dressing
3 T plain non-dry yogurt
3 T orange juice
3 T chopped fresh cilantro or parsley
2 T water
2 T white wine vinegar
2 T lime juice
1 t chili powder
½ onion powder
½ t ground cumin

Combine all ingredients in a covered jar. Shake to mix. Use at once or refrigerate for later use.

Greek Yogurt Tzatziki Salad Dressing

2 cups plain Greek yogurt
1 cup dried seedless cucumber
2 garlic cloves, crushed/paste
1 handful freshly chopped dill
1 handful freshly chopped mint
1 lemon, juiced
Salt and pepper to taste

Let all ingredients sit together for as long as you can wait (a few hours or overnight).

Two Minute Creamy Salad Dressing

Enough for 4 side salads:
2 t Dijon mustard
3 T mayonnaise
2 pinches salt
2 pinches sugar
fresh pepper to taste
1 T Champagne vinegar

Whisk together the mustard, mayonnaise, salt, sugar, and pepper until combined. Add the vinegar and whisk until smooth. Toss with salad greens and serve.

Notes

Notes

Other Cookbooks by Dr. Lund

101 Favorite Freshwater Fish Recipes

Gourmet Freshwater Fish Recipes

101 Favorite Wild Rice Recipes

150 Ways to Enjoy Potatoes

Camp Cooking, Made Easy and Fun

Cooking Minnesotan

The Soup Cookbook

The Scandinavian Cookbook

German Home Cooking

Italian Home Cooking

Eating Green and Loving

100 Favorite Dessert Reci